GOD
AND THE
MACHINE

God and the Machine
Navigating Faith in the Age of AI

God and the Machine

978-1-7910-4106-9

978-1-7910-4107-6 eBook

God and the Machine: Leader Guide

978-1-7910-4108-3

978-1-7910-4109-0 eBook

NATHAN WEBB

GOD
AND THE
MACHINE

NAVIGATING FAITH
IN THE AGE OF AI

ABINGDON PRESS | NASHVILLE

God and the Machine
Navigating Faith in the Age of AI

Library of Congress Control Number: 2025949831
978-1-7910-4106-9

Cover description: On a red background filled with faint binary code, a human hand and a robotic hand reach toward each other, nearly touching. The title "God and the Machine" appears in large white letters, with the author's name "Nathan Webb" and the subtitle "Navigating Faith in the Age of AI" in yellow.

MANUFACTURED IN THE
UNITED STATES OF AMERICA

CONTENTS

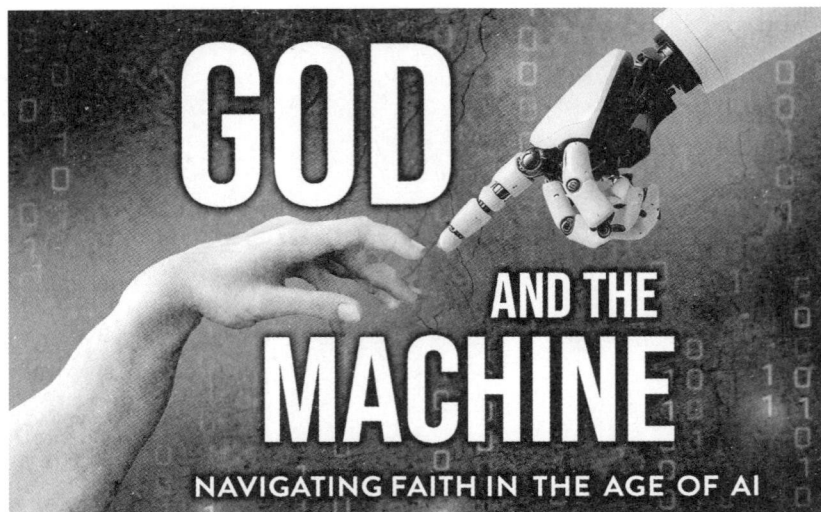

GOD
AND THE
MACHINE
NAVIGATING FAITH IN THE AGE OF AI

Enjoy a short video message from
the author for each chapter of
God and the Machine:
Navigating Faith in the Age of AI.
Great for launching small-group discussion!

Scan the QR code above or visit
https://bit.ly/godandthemachinevideos

Introduction

In 2020, a company called OpenAI unveiled to the world its third generative pre-trained transformer (GPT), named GPT-3. This is a tool trained on vast amounts of text in order to create humanlike text responses of its own. Think of it like the words that pop up as suggestions on your phone, predicting the next word you might want to use in a sentence based on what you and others typically say. For instance, when I type in, "The dog is," the predictive text program will offer suggestions, most likely finishing the sentence with something like "cute." GPT-3 does effectively the same thing but on an exponentially larger scale. You could type in, "Write a Beatles song about my cute dog," and it would oblige with custom lyrics, entirely developed with predictive generation. But this was only the beginning. The capability of AI to generate went beyond text and would soon allow for it to be applied to image, video, and music creation. The possibilities quickly went from text-based to novelty to seemingly endless generative capacity in all forms of media. The same technology could also be used to create the music in the song as well as album cover art and photos of, say, Ringo Starr playing with Lassie.

Up until this point in 2020, I had played with what was becoming colloquially called AI (artificial intelligence) very little. With the debut of GPT-3, which was supposedly more advanced than just about anything that had come before, my curiosity was piqued. I have been similarly gung ho about burgeoning technology in my life and ministry. Being a lifelong nerd, my passion has always been playing with the newest palm pilot or video game console or launching a YouTube channel. I was always the first to try out a new social media platform and see what it was all about—even knowing that it would inevitably be a flop like most of them. I make a hobby of sitting in on the Apple events online and researching what tech leaders are exploring, from VR to wearable tech devices. All things considered, exploring a new digital toy from the comfort of my living room sounded like a blast. I dove headfirst into the fray, testing the program's possibilities for mass content creation, image generation, and file organization.

Experimenting with this kind of new technology is, in some significant ways, part of my job as a pastor. While all ministers have to grapple with whether and how to use new technologies in their work, I am an in a special position as an ordained United Methodist elder serving a digital-first congregation, Checkpoint Church. In many ways, it's probably not so different from most other Methodist churches—prayer, sermons, Bibles, community, music, and everything else that goes with church—except that we don't have a physical building we all meet in. Checkpoint Church explicitly seeks to reach out to nerds, geeks, and gamers—that is, people who often refer to themselves as "digital natives," who are often living at the forefront of the internet, technology, and pop culture. In order to relate to my congregation about these things, and to be able to discover new ways to reach out to like-minded people, I need to stay on top of the latest tech developments. This is the air I breathe, so it's a natural fit for me.

Being a pastor who serves a digital-first congregation, a majority of my work is administrative and mostly involves social media management. This is important work for reaching new people, but it can also take a lot of time and draw my attention away from the more essential work of relationship building. I asked ChatGPT to write some promotional posts and event descriptions and—in a matter of seconds—I had a blurb that sounded just as good as anything I might have written, if not better. I was impressed.

Then, I tried to create images, which was a much different experience, to say the least. I was quickly disappointed to learn that it failed miserably at creating recognizable words or letters. The result was often an invented mishmash of symbols that, at best, looked kind of like recognizable letters if you squinted hard enough. Imagine if you were attempting to re-create an alphabet of a language you had only seen in pictures. But I was impressed by some of the images, so I poked around a bit and rendered some rough logos for designs I was working on. Nothing as impressive as the text generated, but, I thought, *Good enough.*

In 2020, the world was still exploring artificial intelligence. It was a novelty, a party trick of sorts. I recall asking my wife one night if she had heard of GPT. She hadn't, and when I explained it, she brushed it aside and thought of it as being little more than a new Instagram filter or a fad for creating LinkedIn headshots.

Fast forward to 2024, and the world has rapidly adopted AI on a mass scale. Millions of accounts have been created, new models (GPT-4 and 5) have been released to massive success, OpenAI unveiled a paid subscription, and yes, my wife has even created an account of her own. It can feel like something new and groundbreaking happens on a weekly basis, if not daily. A friend of mine wrote a book on artificial intelligence that was released in 2024, and he shared with me that he had a challenge writing it because of just how fast the technology would keep moving. Every time he wrote a chapter and came back to edit, he'd discover that his information was already out of date.

This certainly isn't the first technological breakthrough to take the world by storm. New technologies have always been reshaping how we communicate and interact, from the printing press to the postal service to the radio to the television and most recently the internet. Despite some pushback and resistance with each new introduction, the church has always adapted to these new inventions with time. At one point, the church questioned the efficacy of printing Bibles for everyone, but eventually the church came around to seeing how impactful it could be to allow such technology into our lives. The image of the church being behind the times but eventually getting the picture is one that some of us are likely familiar with in our own church leadership environments. But AI seems different. We don't have time to waste.

With the introduction of AI, the world changed faster than with any other new technology I've ever experienced. I've seen buy-in of social media platforms on a massive scale. I've seen the rise of YouTube and Facebook. But OpenAI and its GPT progeny can only be seen as an instant flash-bang success.

This lightning-fast adoption is breathtaking—and terrifying. Large language models now draft sermons, spin up worship graphics, and even simulate pastoral counseling. We've hardly had a moment to breathe between product launches, let alone voice the pastoral warnings echoed in James 1:5: "If any of you is lacking in wisdom, ask God, who gives to all generously and ungrudgingly, and it will be given you." When can we ask God for wisdom if the reality we are confronting changes every time we turn around? Since 2021, we keep quickly finding ourselves wrapped up in the speed of rapid change without a concern for how much wisdom we have about the holy approach to applying each new iteration of this technology.

Every breakthrough invites blessing and danger. Even in my early days of toying with AI, this has been my prophetic warning: we must see this as the double-edged sword that it is. For example, a large language model can be an incredible asset for ministry. It can generate devotional content in seconds. To be frank, it can generate a whole book of devotions quicker than we can even draft an outline for one. It can translate a sermon into multiple languages in a moment. I now have the ability to dub my voice on YouTube in several different languages at the press of a button. On Instagram, it even tries to match my intonation!

However, it can also be manipulated to provide shallow counseling advice. It offers inaccurate quotations and Scriptures that are entirely made up. We'll dive into this more in later chapters, but *hallucinations* refer to instances when the predictive model confidently makes things up, such as suggesting there is a twenty-fifth chapter of the Gospel of Luke (you can check and see if I hallucinated just then or not). It oscillates between the two extremes of blessing and danger incessantly. So, yes, I've been on the cutting edge of this technology but also pointing out that the cutting edge may slice us back if we aren't careful.

Such warnings are especially important now that AI has become ubiquitous. Of course, not everyone uses it today. But its adoption seems to be growing at a pace that indicates it may be one of those technologies that at first seemed to be an intriguing fad and then becomes something we can't imagine life without. Regardless of how close we might find ourselves in it now, there is no denying that it isn't just a trend or a passing phase. As many of my peers like to say, this technology is currently the worst it will ever be; it's only growing and learning as the world turns. Whatever we conceive of today is just the beginning of where we are headed. In other words, you can't put the genie back in the bottle.

THE CHURCH AS STEWARDS OF ARTIFICIAL INTELLIGENCE

Given this new reality we find ourselves in, the church must care about it. And as leaders in the church, we must be willing to talk about it. We cannot and must not ignore AI. As someone who has seen the cultural deficit that results from the church ignoring nerd-oriented pastimes, and even demonizing them in the era of the satanic panic of the '80s and '90s, we don't have the luxury of decades of faithful nerds who are willing to find their way back to church. When we ask questions about AI, our focus can't be just on future years, let alone decades. Rather, our focus has to be on the here and now.

That is the goal of this study. If the church continues to treat artificial intelligence as *just* a novelty—or *just* a threat—we'll squander the greatest missional opportunity since the advent of the printing press and creation of the World Wide Web. I hope to explore not only the nature of AI and the role it can play in religion but also the guiding role that the church must play before the use of AI leads to negative consequences we could have prevented by asking more complex questions and holding ourselves and these technologies to higher standards. Imagine if Paul had ignored the Roman roads because he was done learning about and using such newfangled technology. The church has played a role in each new communication technology, from the radio to the television to the internet; so we should consider what it would look like for us to carry the mantle when it comes to AI.

I'm not approaching this topic from a place of blind optimism. In fact, since my foray into the technology in 2020, I've been one of the thorns in the side of my more AI-forward mentors. In every gathering and discussion, I'm right there beside them in the space, asking tough questions about the ethics of our work. Since the new AI smell wore off years ago, I've been skeptical about how this technology is and can be used. I believe it can quickly be taken advantage of and misused by those both outside and within the church.

We'll explore some of these examples later. But I want to at least provide some insight into how I'll be approaching the topic. If you're here to hear about the wonder of artificial intelligence, there are plenty of spaces for that. I am much more interested in how the divine is moving amid technology than I am in how to apply it to make our lives more convenient.

I am also not opposed to AI. I avidly use and experiment with many different platforms. I've done start-ups. I've launched apps. I've even done some playful "vibe-coding," where I explain apps with words and the intelligence model does the coding part. Most of the implementations of AI have been unhelpful, and I've left them behind. But I would be remiss if I did not express the massive benefit a proper, healthy implementation can provide. While there is a myriad of moral quandaries to be explored (many of which will be in this book), my experience tells me not to throw the baby out with the bathwater.

As you can glean from my sense of urgency that the church must take this seriously, I think ignoring AI is a serious mistake. That being said, if you're here to hear about the disaster of artificial intelligence, again, there are plenty of places for that. You needn't go far to find a doomsayer. I am much more interested in allowing the divine space to breathe in technology than attempting to gatekeep it from ever trying.

What does it mean to treat AI like an extension of the way that God works in the world? What if we allow it to be incorporated into the means of grace that allows for a wider reach than we thought possible?

One way we might approach this is to consider the commission put on humanity upon their exile from Eden in Genesis 1:28: "God blessed them, and God said to them, 'Be fruitful and multiply and fill the earth and subdue it and have dominion over the fish of the sea and over the birds of the air and over every living thing that moves upon the earth.'" Humankind is given dominion over the land, from flora to fauna to homestead. It may feel like a leap to put that label on artificial intelligence, but what else is technology than human-made provision? In the next chapter, we will define technology more specifically, but for our purposes here we can say it is just how we achieve our goals. It's a tool, like the tools that the earliest humans would have used to till the ground, care for livestock, and raise their families. But we should care about the tools we use and the way that we use them, as this was a task commissioned to humanity in Genesis.

GROUNDED IN LOVE OF GOD AND NEIGHBOR

My starting point for exploring artificial intelligence is grounded in the two greatest commandments offered by Jesus: love of God and love of neighbor. This is not only the lens that I view my faith from, but also one that I think will prove quite valuable for understanding AI.

When Jesus is approached in the Gospel of Matthew by the Pharisees, they devise a trick question to test him: "One of them, an expert in the law, asked him a question to test him. 'Teacher, which commandment in the law is the greatest?'" (22:35-36). We learn that this was a premeditated assault on Jesus's credibility as a leader. Jesus had established some credibility by this time in the Gospel, and the religious authorities needed some way to bring him down a few rungs. This was not a question asked in earnest but was meant to trap Jesus with whatever response he might offer. I have been in a similar spot when my children ask which of them is my favorite. And I only have two! Imagine being forced to choose between 613 commandments. Would Jesus align with the Sabbath-prioritizing leaders we see in other passages calling out Jesus and his disciples? All the Pharisees had to do was get Jesus to pick a side so that they could leverage the other end of the spectrum against him. No matter what Jesus might say, some subgroup would be enraged at Jesus, so it was a no-win situation.

They had actually already tried to trick him earlier in the chapter with a question about the authority of Caesar and whether they ought to pay taxes (a dubious question in any political climate). "Teacher, we know that you are sincere, and teach the way of God in accordance with truth, and show deference to no one, for you do not regard people with partiality. Tell us, then, what you think. Is it lawful to pay taxes to Caesar or not?" (Matthew 22:16-17). Say yes and Jesus looks like a Roman sympathizer who has no problem giving money to the emperor who had conquered his people. Say no and he looks like a political agitator. Jesus's reply is shrewd, designed to satisfy both sides: "Give therefore to Caesar the things that are Caesar's and to God the things that are God's" (v. 21). He suggests they should pay taxes, but perhaps that is just because Caesar's head is on the coins. And what things are God's? All things. Jesus didn't fall for the trap then, and he doesn't fall for this greatest commandment one, either.

Jesus illumines the truth that all the Law and Prophets hang upon the love of God and neighbor. Like my daughter, who refuses to pick a favorite color and just says, "Rainbow," Jesus reveals a deeper truth about how this works on a macro scale. This isn't Jesus being coy or reductive, but instead it is an illustration of the trickle-down effect that happens with two radical commandments being followed.

Love of God and neighbor are also the two things that are most at stake when we do the challenging work of wrestling with any dilemma from a Christian perspective, including technology like artificial intelligence. It's perfectly appropriate that we use Scripture as our lens as Christians seeking out proper discernment for the application of technology, with love of God and neighbor as the heartbeat of the entire Bible. But what would that actually look like?

Since the early days of AI image generation, I have been concerned about those I see called to professional ministry sharing AI-rendered images wantonly. There is one church leader whom I follow online who frequently dissents on digital ministry as an unsatisfactory form of church. Yet, they use AI-generated images in each of their posts. It's not hard to see an AI image and its flaws. Misspelled words, fuzzy rendering, an excess of fingers or limbs on a body. It's sloppy work. This signals a disconnect between faith leaders and their actions, as well as their professed values of digital ethics. Consider that what we do, especially in public-facing worship services, is seen as a kind of tacit condoning of a practice. We are potentially offering a kind of catechesis—an education of how to use AI by how we use AI.

In another instance, church leaders have not paid attention to the dissenting voices speaking about job loss, legal loopholes, and art theft from our fellow human beings. Imagine a poorly rendered AI sermon graphic cast on a jumbotron while an artist, having trouble securing any commissions, sits in the congregation. While a thoughtfully crafted image can be effective for someone who cannot afford to pay an artist, there is no excuse for the careless, purposeless meme-sharing of image generation that occurs in the eyeline of artists struggling to survive. When artificial intelligence is appropriately used, it can bring about ample time-saving that allows for the good, important work of relational ministry.

My fear with image generation is that it seems less focused on that specific benefit and instead does the opposite. It becomes a time-consuming toy that actually risks harm to relationships with artists and creatives in our churches and beyond. There is nuance in any situation, but creating an action figure of yourself broadly benefits no one (this was a particularly egregious trend in the AI world). I can recall during the height of this trend when artists were creating their own action figure renderings as a protest to the AI generations. They were attempting to communicate that they are capable of doing this work too. Even if no one would think to commission an artist for something as silly as making an action figure of themselves, perhaps that was kind of the point—had anyone actually even considered consulting an artist for it? It is doing harm to certain people who are crying out in distress over their careers and financial futures. When we ignore them, we are not loving our neighbor.

Perhaps most pressing of all, there is much controversy over the way that these images are being obtained. At best, consent is very unclear when it comes to the way that the AI models are being trained. Were the artists consulted? Were the images responsibly purchased? How comfortable are we with benefitting from possible exploitation in the church? I am hopeful that much more work will be done here by those who have the power to effect change in the bigger picture; but I am convinced that image generation is something we should not take lightly.

However, when we frame our actions and innovations with these two greatest commandments in mind, we will find that transformation is possible through the gift of technology. We have seen the printing press; the same printing press that made Scripture readily accessible to the masses also made propaganda accessible. We have seen the television, the same television that would cast out powerful testimonies would also host scams and hoaxes of religious con artists. And we have seen the World Wide Web, the same internet that connected the world has also accelerated misinformation at a rate previously unimaginable. Each of these can be used for faithful pursuits that allow us to better love God and neighbor. We have seen the blessings possible with each, as well as the risk.

Another thing that will be noted throughout this book is that the idea of a new technology disrupting the status quo isn't really as new as it seems. AI is certainly an outlier, especially considering how rapidly it has spread and the rate that it accelerates our capacity, but it's not so foreign that we haven't ever experienced such shifts in the church. We know the power of innovation and technology. Without the capacity for widespread printing, how would the *Book of Common Prayer* have been distributed and applied in worship services? Technology has long molded our liturgies and how we use them; AI is simply the latest example. And, as people of faith, we must always challenge ourselves to live up to a higher standard of ethics and discernment about these kinds of fast-moving developments.

As I write this book, my wife has returned to school to pursue a master's degree. We often discuss the challenge of being in a classroom during the rise of AI. You may recall from earlier in this chapter that she wondered if AI might be a fad just a few years ago, but now she is grappling with how to incorporate it into her daily scholastic endeavors. Some of her usage of AI has become so second nature that she has to make sure to stop and consider what a genuinely ethical use might be. I have even caught myself asking ChatGPT to help point me down the right aisle in the grocery store rather than just going and seeking it out myself. Simply because something can be done does not mean that it always should, of course. As Paul says in 1 Corinthians 10:23, "Not all things are beneficial," so discernment is necessary. We must be willing to explore the ethics in what we do as the church. In fact, I believe that is precisely what we're *called* to do.

In chapter 1, we will do the work of establishing definitions and parameters for the world we are working in. The ever-growing list of terms related to artificial intelligence can make this book obsolete overnight, so I will instead try to use broad terms that are likely to remain constant throughout the innovation we will no doubt keep seeing.

Chapter 2 will ground the spiritual part of artificial intelligence. What part does God play in the story we are telling there? How do human beings interact with it in a way that is life-giving and not draining? How do we honor those who are afraid of this technology without being ignorant of its benefits for good ministry?

Then in chapter 3 we will follow up on the work done in the previous chapter with a recommended starting point for engaging with artificial intelligence in a responsible way, exploring some of the ways it is already making an impact. This will be a more practical take on the question of how the church should work with AI effectively.

In chapter 4, we will establish the importance of ethics in the conversation around artificial intelligence by allowing it to be the driving factor, not an afterthought.

Chapter 5 will take a step back and yet deeper into how artificial intelligence changes the way that we will understand and interact with the universal church as well as the local church by reminding us what we mean when we talk about church. We will do this by first analyzing what it even means to be the church in a digital era.

And then the final chapter will offer some insight into future thinking around artificial intelligence. How should we continue doing this work, taking into consideration embodiment and our nascent awareness of where the technology is headed?

This is holy work. A work set apart. It's exciting but also daunting. AI is a hot-button topic for many. For some in the congregation that I serve, AI brings about intense anxiety. That only incentivizes me to further understand it. And is imperative that I do this work with the lens of faith, with the teachings of Jesus at the forefront of my mind. The divine has navigated printing presses, radios, the Web, and much else. It can navigate AI too. And we ought to begin this work sooner rather than later, because once again, artificial intelligence is currently the worst it will ever be; it will only be better tomorrow. Let us journey together and find the Holy Ghost in the machine.

CHAPTER 1

WHAT IS AI, REALLY?

CHAPTER 1

What Is AI, Really?

What comes to mind when you hear the term AI?

Maybe Haley Joel Osment and Steven Spielberg from the movie *A.I. Artificial Intelligence?* HAL-9000 from *2001: A Space Odyssey?* The Terminator? Or Siri and Alexa?

Perhaps we think of the automated voice showing up in more and more facets of our lives—if you're in the Southeast US, you might have heard an AI-generated voice popping up in the drive-thru at the Bojangles or Krispy Kreme. Personally, that's the one I've had the toughest time reckoning with in real life.

And what about the moral qualities we might ascribe to AI programs? Do you picture something evil? Something mysterious whose intentions are unknown? Or do you picture something that is inherently pure and innocent?

In our collective imagination, it is hard to deny that pop culture has played a meaningful role in shaping how we understand the approaching future of artificial intelligence. Most of this fiction, for example the *Terminator* series mentioned above, has been dystopian and has led to a general skepticism toward the possibilities. Would any of us really choose to live in the high-tech hellscape that Hollywood has so often painted this future out to be?

The broader church has certainly not been much help here—the institution itself is most often skeptical toward technology for a few decades until it comes around to incorporating it. Despite our trepidation, we can choose to push the tide forward as religious cultural leaders. But in order to do that work, we must operate within a technologically savvy paradigm. Like Paul, I believe it is essential that we explore things like this in common terms before broaching a deeper dialogue about it; we ought to consume milk before solid food (1 Corinthians 3:2).

As we seek out a definition for artificial intelligence, it may help to ground ourselves first in what a working definition might be for *technology* itself. In the simplest terms, technology is knowledge that is applied in order to satisfy a goal. So, we have three major elements: some kind of knowledge, some kind of application, and some kind of goal.

When we think about technology in this way, it broadens the scope of what we usually count as a technological innovation. A watering can is technology. The goal is watering plants. The knowledge is crafting a container to hold water with a spout that has holes to release the water. Then, the application is watering the plants with the watering can. This goes all the way up to coding lines of ones and zeroes to solve mathematical equations that cause the mysterious black boxes in our pockets to function properly. Technology is what knowledge looks like when it's applied to achieving a goal.

But what does this mean for AI? It's important to understand that the term AI itself is a colloquialism. We are using the term in a nuanced and modernized, yet unspecific, way. When you imagine robots with high intelligence, machines that think and act on their own, you're closer to the mythic AGI, that is, artificial general intelligence. When you think about the fictional Terminator, you're talking about an artificial neural network, a re-creation of the human brain. None of our fictional portrayals of AI are helpful for us to use as a basis for a working definition of the real-world AI we have now. While the label "AI" has stuck and is unlikely to change anytime soon, it's best to think of it as a new and broad concept rather than one directly tied to the historic sci-fi imaginings of artificial intelligence.

When I think about artificial intelligence, I typically don't start with the most technical definition. I start with how it feels in practice—how I actually use it in my day-to-day life. In this vein, a general consideration of AI could be any digital interface that can receive human input and produce a computed response. Note the passing similarity to the textbook definition of technology; the application of knowledge that leads to a goal. But specifically, it's a *digital* knowledge with *algorithmic* application leading to an automated goal. These are the defining factors that help me in determining the broad strokes that make up AI.

In fewer words, it's a digital system that can contemplate, in its own way, and then respond. That might not be the most rigorous scientific definition, but it's where I often land as a digital pastor navigating these tools in real time.

Perhaps you think I might be complicating things unnecessarily. Is this all just semantics? But recall in the introduction, where I stated how contentious artificial intelligence use has become in various spaces, like creative communities. It's likely that the creative person has little issue with a smartphone assistant but would have huge problems with a platform like Midjourney, which is specifically a generative model of artificial intelligence that creates images from natural language prompts. Many would also see no problem with utilizing ChatGPT for making a grocery list or automating a budgeting spreadsheet but would consider it problematic to use the same company's (OpenAI) product DALL-E, which generates images in a potentially problematic way, especially when an artist would otherwise be employed to create such images.

Truthfully, the deeper concern lies in another aspect of AIs, which is *how* they actually get their information. Consider your YouTube recommendation feed—what the algorithm does on that platform. This is the list of videos that the platform offers you to watch next. It is pulling from a resource set filled with *your* specific preferences based on what you have watched and subscribe to. Or perhaps you have a smart plug in your home—one of those fancy switches that allows you to control the lights in your house via a smart assistant like Amazon's Alexa. These are forms of *reactionary* artificial intelligence. They react to stimuli to achieve simple goals. There is no processing beyond readily available inputs. No artificial "thinking." I doubt there are many opposed to the most common instances of this type of intelligence.

Things get more problematic with LLMs (large language models), which require massive amounts of data for training. That is, these AI models are fed massive amounts of text (books, websites, forum posts, documents of all kinds) to allow them to create responses to our prompts. The same also happens with images: image generators are fed huge amounts of art, photos, and graphics so that they can cut and splice all those elements together to generate their own images.

To simplify, the point is that these models are drawing their data from *somewhere*, and decisions about that somewhere must be made by *someone*. When a decision must be made, that means that there can be a myriad of opinions and ethical considerations on how this data is sourced. For instance, there is a litany of copyright holders coming after Midjourney with lawsuits over copyright infringement in the material that was used for the model's image generation. The idea here is that AI platforms are using other people's work, which is then changed, shifted, filtered, and reconfigured to create something. Whether this is similar to how our own minds create anything or if it is simply stealing by another name is an open ethical and legal question. This dilemma is core to the debate over the use and implementation of artificial intelligence in society.

I don't plan to get much further into the minutiae of mechanics of these systems in this book. There are plenty of books out there addressing the bits and bytes, but our goal here is to address how AI and our understanding of it has evolved culturally, especially within Christian culture. For the remainder of this book, whenever I use the term *artificial intelligence*, or *AI*, it is safe to assume that I am referring broadly to the plethora of tools matching the generalized definition I offered above. When needed, I will strive to be specific about the kind of AI I have in mind.

INTERROGATING THOSE BEHIND THE SCENES IN ARTIFICIAL INTELLIGENCE

With an understanding of what artificial intelligence is today, a host of critical questions can now emerge: Who's behind it? Who sets the rules? Who controls the input and output? Who benefits?

If we acknowledge that AI itself is a tool, then our attention ought to be driven to the toolsmith. The relationship between developer and consumer is what highlights the real difference between AI, machine learning, algorithms, and automation. This is also important to us. We should be concerned with the way that technology is stewarded in society. As we understand our Christian role to be good stewards, we ought to own up and step into asking questions of the voices being positioned as authorities.

Take algorithms, for instance—think of social media feeds built and optimized by massive companies like Meta or Google. Or even the TikTok algorithm, which is specifically tuned to show you content that will keep you there the longest. These algorithms are designed to hold attention, often without your explicit consent, and they influence what we see, what we feel, and sometimes what we believe. Whenever I post our weekly nerdy sermons onto YouTube, at the end of the day, I am putting myself at the discretion of that algorithm and the audience it deems worthy of seeing my content. I put in as much work as possible up front, but it is only sent out to the feeds of users that the algorithm decides matches my carefully considered package of information. If I include a word that the algorithm doesn't like, then I will be shoved to the bottom of the pile. In this way, as one might expect in a capitalist society, the developer sets the rules for the mass benefit of a corporation, while the consumer is primarily a passive target audience.

Often, these systems incorporate machine learning, a method for fine-tuning those feeds by designing the system to automatically recognize trends and update its understanding of the best ways to keep users engaged. Again, this is the developer setting the rules, and the result is more hands-off than one might expect.

Automation, on the other hand, is something we can (and often must) set up ourselves. It's intentional and sought out. It's a tool that's given to us with the freedom to use it how we choose. The developer hands over the reins, usually for a price, to allow the consumer to establish a system that benefits themselves. For instance, I've found the intentional use of automation to be a life-changing step when it comes to time and financial management. One of the tools I use daily is called Motion, and it allows for me to sync all of my tasks and meetings to my calendar. When I complete a task, or when something is added that is of a higher priority than existing tasks, then my entire schedule is reassembled by an AI into a new, constantly updating workflow. This allows for me to be more accountable while also maximizing the amount of things that can reasonably be done and scheduled. Once I purchased the license to use the program, the developers offered some tutorials, but it was mostly put on me to set everything up within their framework.

In all of these examples, there is a clear balance between the provider and the consumer, and how they benefit from a day-to-day use of digital technology. Consider the questions above: making that distinction—who builds the tool and who it serves—is crucial to the work set before the church when it comes to our use of technology. It's a work of wisdom and discernment. Automations are self-propelled and don't draw too much concern but can be effective tools. However, when a company like TikTok is able to masterfully maintain the attention of people, we need to be curious about why that is. Perhaps we should suggest prudence in these cases. Sometimes we may even suggest abstinence from these addictive systems. But that isn't to suggest that the option to ignore it all entirely is best or even possible.

We're already interacting with artificial intelligence on a constant basis. As I type this into my word processor, I am receiving automated responses checking my spelling and my grammar. I am also seeing an automated cloud update saving my work online. When my phone rings, my cell phone is capable of scanning the phone number and searching online to see if it is likely to be a scam call or not. Whether it's voice assistants like Alexa, smart recommendations on Netflix, or predictive text on our phones, these systems are embedded into our daily rhythms. Most people don't realize how surrounded by it they already are. The skeptical side of my nature would wager that is intentional on the part of developers. At its best, the effect and working of AI is natural and seamless. And that invisibility makes thoughtful engagement even more important.

While I believe the questions about what AI really is and how we should use it are most pressing, there is one contested technical distinction that matters in ministry: the difference between generative and predictive AI. Many will push back and say there is no difference between the two. I'm less interested in the engineering side of things and more focused on the pastoral considerations. So, for our purposes, I understand that distinction to be that predictive AI helps anticipate what's next based on patterns—like a GPS estimating your arrival time—while generative AI creates something conceptually new from a typically much larger dataset, like a chatbot writing a Shakespearean sonnet about the Jolly Green Giant. Ministry intersects with both. Predictive AI might help anticipate spiritual care needs based on attendance data. Generative AI might help write liturgies. We need to understand what we're using and use it well. By this, I also mean that the opposite also matters. We should know what it does so that we know when *not* to use it. Predictive AI should not replace discernment. Generative AI should not replace our voice, consent, or craft. Knowledge is power, and understanding the building blocks of what AI can do helps us understand its best uses in ministry. As the line between the two continues to blur, multimodal (this refers to an AI that can do more than one thing, both generate text *and* images, etc.) tools like OpenAI will make this distinction harder to identify, but we would still be better served by understanding what we actually want the AI to do with our information.

WHAT ARTIFICIAL INTELLIGENCE ISN'T

We now have a working, if not somewhat simplistic, definition of AI and a better idea of how developers play into the equation. Before we go any further, we have to dispel some common misconceptions.

Q: Is artificial intelligence actually beneficial?

Many folks in church spaces still see artificial intelligence as either a cheap shortcut or a novelty—just funny filters or childish entertainment. AI is also a tool of productivity, persuasion, and sometimes manipulation. It's more than a toy. Like I tell my oldest child when she picks up one of my tools, we have to be careful with it, even if it looks like fun. If we don't take this tool seriously, we risk letting it reshape our ministries without our noticing. There is no denying its prevalence in our culture going forward. Many of us may only interact with it on a surface level, but we should try to develop a deeper understanding of such a powerful new technology.

Q: Should we be afraid of artificial intelligence?

AI triggers strong emotional reactions for a reason. At a core level, we've always been afraid of machines—afraid of what we can't understand, afraid of being replaced, afraid of losing control. That fear runs deep, especially in religious communities that have a long memory of tech-based moral panics. Just in my own thirty-something years of life, I've seen things from credit cards being labeled as the mark of the beast to "satanic" VHS tapes to fears around implantable microchips.

With proper pastoral insight, these concerns are easily brushed away. We aren't people of fear. Even when faced with a future that we cannot possibly predict, Jesus's words in John 14:27 can resound in our hearts, "Peace I leave with you; my peace I give to you. I do not give to you as the world gives. Do not let your hearts be troubled, and do not let them be afraid." We are not meant to live in fear of any coming technology, but instead we are to embody the gift of Christlike peace for ourselves and those around us.

As we've already explored, science fiction has played a major role in shaping public imagination—Christian or otherwise. Stories from *The Matrix* to *Black Mirror* color how we imagine the future of artificial intelligence. We expect dystopia. We anticipate the apocalypse. And for many Christians, that defaults to suspicion or panic. As a practitioner of digital ministry, I often have *Snow Crash*, a dystopian fiction book about virtual reality, foisted into any argument about the merit of digital churches. We let our imagination be guided by the creative works we consume.

But I see a range of postures in the church. Older members may feel suspicious or just totally disengaged. Meanwhile, many pastors seem to see AI as a shortcut to greater influence, making them more effective and efficient. The professionalization of ministry can become a driver for optimization. That desire isn't impure, but without discernment, it becomes dangerous.

What the church most needs to confront is the wanton, unthinking use of artificial intelligence. We must build an ethical backbone before we get swept up in the next wave of tech enthusiasm. Otherwise, we'll find ourselves accelerating faster than our values can keep up.

But the deeper concern I carry isn't just fear. It's that we're not asking the preemptive ethical questions. We're rushing to use AI because it's flashy and useful—but we're not always asking if we should, or how we ought to. It can often feel that AI creation and usage is a bit like Jeff Goldblum's foreboding warning in *Jurassic Park*—we're so concerned with what we can do that we've forgotten to ask if we should. Maybe a more Pauline take might be that all things may be lawful, but not everything is beneficial (1 Corinthians 10:23). Or in a Wesleyan spirit, we should not only consider how to avoid harm but also how to actively do good. And it's that lack of reflection on the part of hungry leaders that worries me more than the technology itself.

Q: So, is AI just a tool or something more spiritually significant?

I believe that AI is unquestionably a tool. But the way we use it—what we pour into it, what we do with the outputs—that's where the spiritual dimension emerges. Tools aren't neutral once they're in motion. A hammer can build or harm. If I use a hammer to build a birdhouse, then I will likely produce a beautiful result. If I use a hammer to dust my television screen, then I'll be making a trip to the electronics store later. Artificial intelligence is much the same: spiritually neutral while being ethically charged. We should be concerned with the application of it so that we know the best way forward (and prevent accidents and misuses from happening in advance).

Q: Can AI reflect God's image?

AI itself does not bear the *imago Dei* (image of God). We must dispel this notion often and firmly. This human tendency to anthropomorphize technology isn't a faithful and honest stewardship of the technology we've been given. Here's an example of what I mean. A few years ago, I was given an automated vacuum for my birthday. I chose to name the robot Alfred, as an allusion to the butler for my favorite bat-themed superhero. My wife and I would dotingly refer to the vacuum using male pronouns.

Reflecting on that, I'm innocently anthropomorphizing, that is, ascribing human characteristics to something nonhuman. Many of us make a habit of doing this with our technology.

There's a real danger, though, in anthropomorphizing AI—treating it like a person. Perhaps you've stumbled upon the live stream of an AI representation of Jesus that is trained on Scripture and answers questions. For the most part, many of the questions asked are absurd or inconsequential, but there is a temptation to see this virtual homage to Jesus as more than it is: code. We never treated the printing press or the typewriter as human, so why do we feel differently about artificial intelligence? Maybe because it talks back. Maybe because it seems to "know" us. But we need to be clear-eyed and stalwart: this is powerful software, not a soul.

However, I do believe artificial intelligence can reflect *our* image—and, by extension, reflect our bearing of the image of God. The art we render with AI, the systems we train, and the stories we tell all reflect our creativity. If we believe that our creativity reflects our Creator, then yes, I believe artificial intelligence can be part of that echo, even if it's a few steps removed.

The early church offers helpful parallels. Paul's letters were a kind of tech-enabled communication, made possible by advances in transportation, paper, and writing technology. Today, AI could be the same: a delivery system for the gospel. However, we must also remember that mass printing has enabled harmful tools, such as Chick Tracts, which often steered toward questionable ideologies shoved into a religious guise. Or what about the endless spam mail that arrives in our mailboxes warning us about our vehicle's extended warranty? AI could become our next Chick Tract or spam mail moment if we don't discern its power. When everyone has the power of mass creation, that includes both good and ill-minded actors.

Biblically, the Great Commission comes to mind. After years of ministry, being crucified, and then raised from the dead, Jesus meets with the eleven disciples and sends them out to share the bold message of the gospel. He commissions them by proclaiming, "All authority in heaven and on earth has been given to me. Go therefore and make disciples of all nations, baptizing them in the name of the Father and of the Son and of the Holy Spirit and teaching them to obey everything that I have commanded you. And remember, I am with you always, to the end of the age" (Matthew 28:18-20). We have inherited this ancient commission to make disciples far and wide. In the digital age, those nations include the gathered populace of the online world. Who are we to decide that AI should be the thing we *don't* implement to further the mission of the church? If artificial intelligence becomes a tool to reach new people, we should use it. But with care.

Q: What does the church stand to gain by embracing AI thoughtfully?

With an open mind and an ethical heart, the possibilities seem limitless. We can expand our reach. We can automate repetitive tasks, allowing us to focus more on the relational aspects. We can tell stories better. We can create with excellence. We can minister more personally because we've freed up bandwidth to be present.

As mentioned in an earlier portion of this book, I am a frequent user of AI. On a daily basis, I will use it to offer up invaluable insight into data around my congregation. I have an automation with ChatGPT that provides me with three ideas for stimulating an online forum with questions, thoughts, or insights from that week's sermon.

One of my favorite implementations of artificial intelligence has been making the massive amount of content that I create more accessible. For example, AI can provide descriptions that can be applied to images online for those with impaired vision. Modern devices are equipped with screen readers that can read aloud these descriptions, making our content available to a wider audience that often goes unnoticed.

Another application is translating the captions of our videos—a process now automated by YouTube. Whenever I upload a nerdy sermon onto our YouTube channel, it will use AI to automate the captions and then generate an artificial version of my voice in several different languages, meaning that—without any extra work from me—I now create video content that can share the gospel with exponentially more people.

But all of that hinges on discernment. The greatest danger is using artificial intelligence recklessly—full speed with no brakes, no map. That's not innovation. That's chaos.

AI ON ITS OWN TERMS

If you've taken the time to explore the world of AI, then this will not come as a shock to you, but it won't take long for you to discover that it isn't magic. It's amazing and fast, but it's far from a genie in a bottle. When I first began toying with AI, I would have it write parody versions of the top-charting songs on a guitar chord website. This was done in an attempt to make our weekly announcements a bit fresher and stick in people's memories longer. What pastor hasn't lamented that feeling when no one knows anything in the bulletin? I would provide it with the events of the coming week so I could offer up our news in a more creative light.

The songs were terrible.

It often missed the syllabic structure of the original rhyme scheme or just made up details about one of our events that made no sense. While it was a funny idea, the actual implementation of it was a flop. Context is king, and we weren't providing the AI model with the right amount of context. We tried something new and found that our inputs, mixed with hallucination on the AI's part, turned out to be a poor concoction. The real lesson here is that artificial intelligence will not give automatically perfect results—it takes work to get it right. This applies to the way that the church is using it too.

AI isn't evil. It's not alive. It's not demonic. It's a tool. But like any tool, it needs ethical guidance. That's why it matters how we use it—and why we need a comprehensive theology of technology, as soon as possible.

I've seen artificial intelligence used poorly in ministry. AI-generated images that look cheap or uncanny. Posts that replace art with algorithmic slop. These aren't just bad aesthetics—they hurt people. They signal to artists that we don't need them. They say, "We'd rather have free content than human creativity." That's a misuse of our calling. We must do better. But where should we start?

We'll dive in a good bit more into the ethical side of the story, but here's a solid footing for our first chapter: start with transparency. Don't hide your AI usage. Talk about it. Teach about it. Make an AI policy. Set boundaries. Use the discomfort as an invitation into conversation.

The truth is that AI is already everywhere. It's embedded. It's accelerating. And if we don't engage now, we'll lose the chance to shape how it can be used for good. It's our responsibility—not just as tech users but as stewards—to name what's happening, to wrestle with it ethically, and to find God within it.

INTERROGATING THOSE BEHIND THE SCENES IN ARTIFICIAL INTELLIGENCE

With an understanding of what artificial intelligence is today, a host of critical questions can now emerge: Who's behind it? Who sets the rules? Who controls the input and output? Who benefits?

If we acknowledge that AI itself is a tool, then our attention ought to be driven to the toolsmith. The relationship between developer and consumer is what highlights the real difference between AI, machine learning, algorithms, and automation. This is also important to us. We should be concerned with the way that technology is stewarded in society. As we understand our Christian role to be good stewards, we ought to own up and step into asking questions of the voices being positioned as authorities.

Take algorithms, for instance—think of social media feeds built and optimized by massive companies like Meta or Google. Or even the TikTok algorithm, which is specifically tuned to show you content that will keep you there the longest. These algorithms are designed to hold attention, often without your explicit consent, and they influence what we see, what we feel, and sometimes what we believe. Whenever I post our weekly nerdy sermons onto YouTube, at the end of the day, I am putting myself at the discretion of that algorithm and the audience it deems worthy of seeing my content. I put in as much work as possible up front, but it is only sent out to the feeds of users that the algorithm decides matches my carefully considered package of information. If I include a word that the algorithm doesn't like, then I will be shoved to the bottom

CHAPTER 2

GENERATED IN WHOSE IMAGE?

introduction, where I stated how contentious artificial intelligence use has become in various spaces, like creative communities. It's likely that the creative person has little issue with a smartphone assistant but would have huge problems with a platform like Midjourney, which is specifically a generative model of artificial intelligence that creates images from natural language prompts. Many would also see no problem with utilizing ChatGPT for making a grocery list or automating a budgeting spreadsheet but would consider it problematic to use the same company's (OpenAI) product DALL-E, which generates images in a potentially problematic way, especially when an artist would otherwise be employed to create such images.

Truthfully, the deeper concern lies in another aspect of AIs, which is how they actually get their information. Consider your YouTube recommendation feed— what the algorithm does on that platform. This is the list of videos that the platform offers you to watch next. It is pulling from a resource set filled with your specific preferences based on what you have watched and subscribe to. Or perhaps you have a smart plug in your home— one of those fancy switches that allows you to control the lights in your house via a smart assistant like Amazon's Alexa. These are forms of reactionary artificial intelligence. They react to stimuli to achieve simple goals. There is no processing beyond readily available inputs. No artificial "thinking." I doubt there are many opposed to the most common instances of this type of intelligence.

Things get more problematic with LLMs (large language models), which require massive amounts of data for training. That is, these AI models are fed massive amounts of text (books,

CHAPTER 2

Generated in Whose Image?

If you've never taken the time to see who is most anxious about the implementation of artificial intelligence in our society, I encourage you to look around at dissenting voices. Find a popular video on AI and then open the comment section. In my experience online, the ones offering the loudest skeptical takes are the ones who are those in creative industries.

I've spent the last five years wrestling with the church over digital ministry, championing everything from Discord servers to Twitch streams. The pushback felt familiar—hesitancy, skepticism, fear of "the new." (I use scare quotes here because the internet is about as new as Chris Tomlin.) But with AI I've noticed a twist: the resistance isn't coming from the old guard this time; it's coming from younger voices worried about losing jobs, creativity, and even the planet. When it's the younger voices who are crying out, it should behoove us to hear what's being said. It's for this reason that, even though I am an early adopter, I have been listening to the voices of those deeply skeptical of this new technology.

As I wade through the waters between tech enthusiast and AI skeptic, I often find myself seeing the laments of a screenwriter who is furious about hearing studio executives planning to use artificial intelligence for an upcoming slate of television shows or the mourning of a visual artist who has been slighted by a peer who decided to use image generation to cut costs. I don't think that this pattern is just a coincidence.

Our *imago Dei* is at stake. And the creatives are feeling that most palpably.

In the previous chapter, we discussed a bit about how the Great Commission of Matthew 28 plays into our role in a digital world with technological tools like artificial intelligence. The truth is that the role of the divine in our ministry work goes back much further than that—all the way to the beginning.

In the first chapter of Genesis, readers are offered an account of God creating the first human beings—flesh from the dust that are made in the likeness of Godself. "Let us make humans in our image" (v. 26), says the divine Creator.

This comes after a litany of creative work by God. In a triumphant buildup to the grand finale, God has sewn together the heavens and the earth. God has illuminated everything with light and then shrouded some parts with darkness. God has formed the waters of the sky and the waters below and caused dry land to sprout from beneath it. God exploded that ground with greenery and foliage, blooming and blossoming from the empty wasteland. God then brings about wild animals—majestic and carefree. Sewn, illuminated, formed, exploded, blooming, blossoming—these words indicate that God is a creative force. A whirlwind of passionate formation. It's not wanton creation, but beauty in motion.

And then—after all of this *making*, God makes humankind in God's own image. What image do we have to superimpose on that, given what we've been told so far? Who has God been up until the point where humanity finds our footing? What example could we look to? The answer is clear: God is the *Creator* and created us to be like *that* . . . little creators.

WE WERE CREATED TO CREATE

The act of creation is a holy one. This is a sentiment that resonates with both believers and nonreligious artists. There is a kind of "losing of oneself" in creating art. The jazz singer who finds themselves lost in the melody. The sculptor who doesn't notice the sun setting while they chip away at the hours of the day. Even my own woes and sorrows vanish as I place my calloused fingers upon worn guitar strings, digging into well-trod divots in my fretboard, ascending to a place I can only describe as divine. All of these are ways we commune with something beyond ourselves. Because when we create, we're doing that which we were made to do.

God is the preeminent creator. We echo that notion in every good thing that we create. This is what feeds my theological framing of the sentiments experienced by artists from diverse backgrounds. We embody the image of God when we invest a part of our self—intuition, prayer, imagination—into the act of making. I often use this to explain much of my work and how I see Christian morals being explored in storytelling, whether that be in creative writing, animation, or video games. This is most of what I do in my pastoral work.

I believe that most creatives can see this train of thought, even outside of any structural religious background. The issue that arises that is relevant to artificial intelligence and its distortion of the *imago Dei* comes less from the act of creation and more from the subjective definitions we have of art—and especially when the definition of art is connected to medium. By medium, I mean what we use to make art with. If painting, then oil or minerals. If guitar music, then wood and string. If humanity is art, then dust is the medium. In modern times, tensions are sparked by evolving technology's entrance into the artistic process.

Whenever AI begins to get involved in the process, it seems to reopen old wounds around art in digital mediums being perceived as taboo. I recall a specific subset of creatives who found the early Pixar films appalling due to their computer-generated imagery. Or the critiques of synthesizers not creating an authentic musical experience. As a creative myself, I follow several art influencers online who swear by the tactile feel of a pen on paper, insisting that one only truly begins to feel the flow of art when they have the proper fountain pen on the finest imported paper. Even still, they would sooner see me use a cheap ballpoint pen than consider digital means of creation. Or—closer to my own heart—there is the broader discussion about video games being a form of art worth taking seriously.

All of these things, analog or digital, are by definition acts of creation; but there are groups of creative people that do not define the results as *art*. When we involve technology in any creative act, we risk ringing a hollow note, short-circuiting the image of a creative God that we bear and removing any humanity from it at all. However, even the normative use of technology in an era before deepfakes and AI slop pales in comparison to the mindless churn of image generation when we incorporate artificial intelligence.

For this chapter, I'd like to focus on one specific use of generative artificial intelligence: image generation. It's the use case that I find myself most stubbornly pushing back against. In nearly every other instance of technology invading art mentioned above, I am pushing to welcome digital mediums, but AI has brought about a different response from me. Perhaps it's due to my creative aspirations—I find visual generations to be cheap and not earned. I find them to not live up to my expectations. Or maybe the issue lies in a certain subset of those who use image generation referring to themselves as "AI artists," a loaded and controversial term. That's not to say I have never used any of the tools. In my earlier days of dabbling, I set up an account with Midjourney and attempted to gin up some images that might fit my needs—a cartoon avatar, a four panel comic, a logo or two—but ultimately I found myself unimpressed with the residual sameness of the images. For this reason, I use image and video generation sparingly, if at all.

My argument thus far is that our own creative acts are an extension of our God-bearing image, but a creative action that is prompted for a machine to undertake doesn't feel like divine partnership, and AI generating something without careful consideration seems like irresponsibility on the part of the user. If technology is achieving goals through application of knowledge, then what do we do with a technology that "achieves" art?

The images created by AI aren't *really* creation, but a form of re-creation. It may *seem* so but is not truly new creation. It can be tasteful, and it can even lead to unique forms of imagery. With proper prompting, one can generate a truly unique image—say, a fire hydrant dressed up like a ninja turtle. I'd wager that is bizarre enough to be pretty original. But even then, the assets that the AI program will pull from are all existing pieces of art created by human beings. This art is dissected and reassembled into something different. What is unique is not necessarily new.

What I'm hoping to illustrate here is that artificial intelligence is not, in and of itself, creative. Ascribing creativity to it is another instance of an erroneous anthropomorphizing. It can remix, extrapolate, approximate, and maybe even improvise. But if the image you end up with has any real craft to it, then that says more about the human mind prompting it or, more often than not, editing it post-generation. At its best, image generation is done with strict oversight by human eyes.

THE RESULT OF UNCHECKED ARTIFICIAL INTELLIGENCE

A serious problem with image generation is AI slop. You may not know this term, but you have very likely seen an example of it on your Facebook feed.

Stop me if you've heard this before: an image of a one-legged white Jesus (probably in a robe with a red sash) sitting in a wheelchair, likely holding a sign that says, "It's my birthday," (likely misspelled) and about two hundred comments saying, "Amen," or some similar affirmative phrase.

Or maybe you've caught this one: a few random, bedraggled men in army fatigues helping orphan children out of a burning building onto a plane with Polynesian flight attendants. And it's also probably at least one of the children's or soldier's or flight attendant's birthdays. And they may or may not be missing legs.

But crucially, the comment section must be flooded with affirming religious phrases (again, AMEN!).

This is AI slop. These are examples that happen to have a religious component to them, but slop knows no bounds; it can be about anything or anyone.

What has happened here? A third party has set up an automated code and intelligence system that posts images at a fast pace onto a Facebook page, perhaps a new image every few seconds. The code then interprets the best-performing posts, taking into account who is in the image, what they're wearing, and any miniscule detail an AI can spot, and then the program prioritizes the findings. This creates a feedback loop that spits out an algorithmically-optimized level of images that are specifically tuned to get likes and comments. In a twist of irony, that same third party will often set up fake user accounts to type in positive comments to further boost the ranking. For some reason, Jesus, soldiers, missing limbs, Polynesian flight attendants, and birthdays seem to be among the best candidates for manipulating the system.

These images are not real, of course. But that is the least of the issues with them.

Consider the results of these automations—we cannot ignore that the elements that perform best are often religious in nature. Why is our language being co-opted? Why is the sacred image of Jesus being used for manipulation? We should be taking this seriously, looking for ways to discourage the use and spread of AI slop.

I'm doubtful that much of the slop out there is being produced by those in ministry, but the temptation stands nonetheless. The allure of these AI slop machines is the potential for massive reach.

In many of the AI workshops I've been a part of, there has been a shared interest in creating automations that eliminate the need to ever have to do the work of social media outreach at all—an automation program that will create and post Scripture images to Instagram without any oversight, for example, or using an auto-responding robot to immediately comment on a YouTube channel video. Some of these uses are more utilitarian. Some are more manipulative. Regardless, for pastors, there is a fine line between eliminating mundane work and eliminating meaningful relational work.

For instance, why would we want to have an endless, unmonitored list of Scripture on an Instagram feed? Really consider that question. Best case scenario, you want to reach people with a positive message on their feed. Fair enough. But what if the automation draws out one of the more scandalous verses on accident? What if there is a world event outside of your control that coincides with the passage used inappropriately? In those instances, we risk doing harm to those on our feed.

Regardless of these worst case scenarios, I still wonder if we are asking an honest "why" behind projects like these. How are we living out the call to make disciples by only really servicing an algorithm? That's not to say we cannot and should not play by the algorithmic "rules," but we must be willing and able to ask ourselves these discerning questions. A lack of this honest analysis is what leads to AI slop.

The account of the early church in Corinth brings about an interesting framework for wrestling with this lackluster work. In 1 Corinthians 10:23, Paul is reckoning with the freedom of the believer. He begins his analysis with reports of what he must be hearing from the afflicted church members, "'All things are permitted,' but not all things are beneficial. 'All things are permitted,' but not all things build up." There appears to be some uncertainty about what to do in regard to food. Paul did not advocate that all Christians must follow Jewish dietary laws, but should Christians eat food sacrificed to idols? The Corinthians might have wondered what harm there could be.

Paul is clear that the problem with eating food sacrificed to idols isn't that the idols have real power or that it would violate a person's conscience. Rather, he says, "Do not seek your own advantage but that of the other" (1 Corinthians 10:24). The more pressing matter for Paul is how our actions affect others. We might subject people to temptations or risky behaviors that aren't a problem for us.

This gets to the core of our main thesis about loving God and loving neighbor in our AI ethical code. When we put our focus on how the work we are doing affects ourselves, we miss the forest for the trees. I worry we do this often in our own callings—at least, I am guilty of it in my ministry. Paul encourages us to get down to what really matters: "Whether you eat or drink or whatever you do, do everything for the glory of God. Give no offense to Jews or to Greeks or to the church of God, just as I try to please everyone in everything I do, not seeking my own advantage but that of many, so that they may be saved" (1 Corinthians 10:31-33). AI might make us uncomfortable or at times confused or uncertain, but perhaps it is worth using for the glory of God. And that implies that we ought to use it fully but also ethically, as we would anything done for the glory of God. If it is our commission to make disciples, we ought not cut any corners.

A BETTER PATH FORWARD

We should pursue excellence in our endeavors—with or without AI influence. If you want to be stalwart against AI use, that's fine. Make sure that your work is excellent. If you want to use AI in every project, that's fine. Make sure that your work is excellent.

More than anything, this is a Christian appeal against being lukewarm. To be lukewarm is to be half-hearted in our work done for God. In Revelation, we see the looming fate of the lukewarm: "Because you are lukewarm and neither cold nor hot, I am about to spit you out of my mouth" (3:16). In the Pauline text, we are urged to do everything for the glory of God.

A particularly inspiring example that I hold on to as a creative is Bezalel. That might not be the most familiar Bible character, but it's one that I think about daily.

The story begins in Exodus 25, where we have Moses serving as the middleman between the Lord up on the mountain and the Israelites, who are trying to get their act together. Moses is tasked with dictating the laws and commandments that the Lord has planned for a nation recently emancipated from captivity. Moses ascends Mount Sinai to receive these directions, with the following five chapters of Exodus serving as plans for the projects that he is to tell the nation to create. The Lord lists instructions for a tabernacle so that the Lord might be able to dwell among the Israelites. They also are told to construct an ark for the covenantal law to be housed in. In the instructions, there are specific measurements and expectations for types of wood and oil to use, incense to burn, offerings to be made.

After running through the list, the Lord then tells Moses that there is an Israelite named Bezalel who will be specifically charged with creating these structures and objects. And the Lord also speaks of Oholiab, who will assist Bezalel. But more importantly for our purposes, the Lord explains to Moses that these two have been specifically gifted by the spirit of God to create what God has called for. Bezalel has been granted the wisdom and knowledge to do these things—from cutting stone to working in gold to all other types of handicrafts.

Remember the definition of technology? Bezalel is a technologist! He has been spiritually granted the knowledge that will be applied to achieve certain goals for the nation of Israel by decree of God on Mount Sinai.

Now, imagine if Bezalel heard this call and asked, "Great—now what corners can I cut?" It's a laughable thought. There is no doubt that the work performed by these two and their team was of exceptional quality. They were specifically tasked to do a good work for the Lord, and we should expect that they did their absolute best, just as we would if ordained by God for a particular calling or mission.

And we are all called by God to participate in our churches, to help them be places where God can be found by all people. Still, there is no doubt that churches do not have the proper help for many major tasks. They are understaffed. Pastors are overworked. That kind of pressure can lead anyone to want to take advantage of shortcuts. And I empathize but still vehemently encourage us to pursue excellence in all we do.

One way that we can do this is to build out an AI policy. Having a set of standards is a huge step in forming an adequate response to AI. Here are my suggestions for some foundational work that your church could do in forging an AI policy.

First, make sure you're including other human beings when producing things for the church or broader public. Run documents, social media posts, and other content by fresh sets of eyes. Don't allow the production process to become an island. We miss things that could have been avoided when we don't allow others to have any oversight on our work.

Second, include artists first and foremost. If you can afford the work, then you should pay for it. We should prioritize supporting the *imago Dei* in our creative siblings in Christ before using alternatives.

Finally—and this is a tough one for me—call out AI slop when you see it. Do this kindly and considerately, but remember that it's worth telling someone that their work is clearly derived from AI and could be causing harm. This can be challenging, of course. But take note of what Jesus teaches in Matthew 18:15-17: air your concerns to someone privately before considering bringing in others in the church.

In the next chapter, we will lay out more practical use cases for how we might best use AI—for how we might make our work more excellent for the glory of God. While I hope you take what I have shared here into consideration as you work on your own personal or church's AI policies, it's worth keeping in mind what we know to be true: artificial intelligence will never bear God's image. We do. Every prompt we write, every dataset we approve, every post we publish must therefore echo the Creator—with skill, with empathy, and with holy accountability. Anything less is slop.

DOES GOD USE TECHNOLOGY?

CHAPTER 3
Does God Use Technology?

I was born into a church family. My dad is a second-career pastor who started his new job as a student pastor while in seminary, when I was still in diapers. When he graduated and was moved from his student pastor appointment to his first full-time appointment, he was tasked with entering as the second pastor of a new church plant. He had been tapped because of his managerial and financial experience in his previous work experience—ask any church planter and they will tell you those are key skills.

My sister was just old enough to drive at the time, and so she went undercover to scope out the church and learn if our dad could handle the task. All we had heard was that the church was "contemporary," which our church experience to that point had not been—suits and ties, handbells and organ music—the works, traditionally speaking. A far cry from what we assumed was the no doubt raucous, blasphemous behavior happening at this new church start.

After her quick act of espionage, my sister returned home with a confident air about her. These folks were just good ol' country folks like us. Our dad could handle the job—and he'd even get to wear blue jeans!

We had an image in our heads of smoke machines and a laser light show, but the label of "contemporary" really just meant they had screen projectors and a drum set. We had a misunderstanding, and it nearly kept us from finding out that nothing fundamental or truly important was shifting. Considering where my future path would take me to planting a digital-first church, I'd say that it wound up being a pretty normal church experience, one that was certainly less "contemporary" than where I am now.

TECHNOLOGY NEEDS A DRIVER

Regardless of the era or the technology, the truth of the church (and really any community-driven thing) is that progress moves at the rate of the people who run the show. If you don't have a tech-savvy twelve-year-old, then you might not have anyone to run slides. If you don't have a willing local guitarist, then you might be plugging the organ back in. If no one can figure out the VHS tape player, then you're stuck with puppet shows. The tool only makes a difference when someone knows how to use it.

The people of the church are what makes the whole thing move forward. Remember our definition from earlier: technology is knowledge wisely applied to achieve a goal. It gets nowhere without someone applying that knowledge. This is where we come to God's role in all of this. Can God use technology? Of course, God can do whatever God wants to do. The more logical question might be: *Does* God use technology? Even more specific, does God use *us* to use technology? Again, a resounding yes.

One of the most iconic Bible stories (like, first day in Sunday school) features Noah using the technology of his day to build a behemoth of a boat to survive a coming flood. Knowledge helped build a boat with Noah at the helm to achieve the goal of survival. The spiritual father of Methodism, John Wesley, is known for his prudent use of pamphlets, a technology made possible by the printing press and its continued refinement. The knowledge about ink applied to paper facilitated a field preacher to spread the gospel message.

God has used technology often. We have no shortage of people tasked with sharing the gospel message through technology. The church has been what allows the gift of technology to reach farther and wider than it was thought possible when Jesus commissioned those who stood with him some two thousand years ago.

Whether looking at the example of my father at that contemporary new church or Noah, Paul, or John, the point is that God uses God's people. And, creative beings that we are, God's people are skilled with wisdom in using technology. If we return to the Bezalel example, it could even be argued that the spirit of God imbues the skill to use technology in certain people for the work laid before us.

Is the tool holy? That's not the question. It's just a tool; it's neutral.

Can the tool be useful for spreading God's love? Now we're on the right track.

ARTIFICIAL INTELLIGENCE CAN BE USED FOR GOOD

Today, there is a new tool on the scene, AI, and it feels more powerful than anything that came before it. At least, sort of.

I think AI can often feel much like my own particular calling toward digital ministry—something contested, a bit risky, in some important ways unlike anything we've tried before. But simply because it is new doesn't mean it should be rejected outright. It also doesn't mean that it should be blindly trusted.

I'll offer an example of how I believe that artificial intelligence can be ethically employed in a way that is useful for God. Each week, like most pastors, I sit down for an extended period of time and prepare my sermon. Now, my sermons in particular are an unusual take on the form. I'm a pastor of a church for nerds, geeks, and gamers. My sermons mention superheroes, anime protagonists, and video game mascots. Nevertheless, the core of my work would be familiar to most churchgoers. I do the hard work of exegeting the Scripture for the week. I toil over the commentaries. I dig through the Hebrew and Greek. I sift out the best ideas and consider the context of my congregation. But then the course veers. It comes down to recording. Not only are we a church for nerds, we're also a fully *digital* church. That means every sermon must be filmed and edited professionally—the video isn't just a recording of the "real" service for those who couldn't attend that week; it *is* the service, and the people seeing it on their screens are the entirety of the congregation.

In order for our sermons to reach the most people possible, both our existing congregation as well as digital passersby, we have to consider several factors. We post on YouTube, which hosts our videos and, via its algorithm, decides who else might want to see it in their feed. YouTube wants to find the optimal video for the optimal audience. For creators, this means that we have to fine-tune the videos that we post (and all the data and preferences we include with them) in order for the content to be most easily accessible or, frankly, accessible at all. We do this with a process called search engine optimization (SEO), which attempts to make it so that our videos come at the top of the list when people search for, say, "digital church" or "online Methodist service" or "nerdy church sermon." It's a confusing and constantly evolving scheme. The target of what's best for ranking your content on that algorithm shifts like the tide. Some days it's best to focus on the terms you choose to associate with your video, others it's best to play the thumbnail game (tinkering with the small still images that constitute links to videos), sometimes it matters if the first sentence of your description has the perfect three keywords. As a solo pastor, I don't have the time or bandwidth to relearn proper SEO tactics every week.

Instead, I use AI. After my sermon has been fully crafted and lovingly tuned, I send the manuscript to ChatGPT, along with several other goals and expectations that I have for its performance.

I tell the AI that I'd like a thorough SEO process performed for a video utilizing the provided transcript. I offer insight into our target audience. I tell it what the video will look like and what I hope it delivers on its themes. The AI will then comb through my work, the information that I've fed it, and one other crucial piece of information: the SEO resources I've already provided. I regularly seek out experts in the field of SEO and use their tips and tricks to build the initial AI framework before ever offering the program my work. After all of this, the AI will take a few seconds and return my work to me in a fully fleshed-out SEO report.

It will recommend many different titles and spell out the logic behind each of them. It will have a list of hashtags including the three most highly recommended to use in the description. It will recommend thumbnail images based on what has worked for others in my field. Sometimes, I will even ask the AI to provide me with text to be included in promotional materials to send out with social media posts when it comes time to share the video after it goes live.

While it's a subjective boundary, all of this is well within my understanding of the ethical use of artificial intelligence. We'll dive more into these ethical boundaries in another chapter. For now, I want to point out the importance of starting with good information and prompts and the need for oversight and checking. I've provided the AI with sources and some of my own writing to base its drafts on. All of the reports that it creates are accompanied by a description of its logic, so the program explains any work that it has done so that I can check it over and ensure accuracy. And, most importantly, it is done with a specific and measurable purpose in mind. I'm not just using artificial intelligence for some frivolous purpose or to amuse myself on a slow afternoon; I'm using it to maximize the reach of my church for the purpose of evangelism.

There are a few vital things to note here: (1) I provided the AI with a good amount of information on my end, (2) I laid a framework of expectations, and (3) I held full control of the tool at all times.

If we don't provide AI with plenty of our own work, we will get generic and lackluster responses. We must tell the program what we want it to do, and more specific instruction is almost always better. If you want the AI to write or create something for you, give it relevant samples. Most of the developers have become savvy to this and even provide the option to have the responses solely based on the information that you provided.

Even those who profit from this technology can recognize that AI shouldn't be doing all the work for you but rather doing it with you. The alternative is a lazy and uninspired output. I had a mentor who always said, "It is not garbage in, garbage out. It is garbage in, garbage stays." When we fail to put in the initial effort, we set AI (and ourselves) up for disaster. Continuing with our tool metaphor, this would be like using a drill to place a nail in the wall. Or, perhaps even lazier, it is like setting a drill and a nail next to each other and expecting them to finish the job without needing your help. We have to provide the tool with the proper material to ensure that what is done is not just acceptable, but exceptional.

Not only do the results suffer when we don't take an active role when using AI, but this amounts to a lack of consideration of our relationship with AI. If we don't provide a framework of expectations, then we are allowing the computer program to hold too much of the power. For example, as noted, I make a lot of video content for YouTube. Now, there are a lot of YouTube channels out there. I don't want my sermons to be marketed like a MrBeast—a popular YouTube content creator—video. MrBeast is known for philanthropic ventures, so there's a chance that an AI could try to use his techniques for my content, but I can offer deeper perspective into how my intentions diverge from the reality television style of MrBeast's videos. We have different goals, target audiences, and styles. MrBeast is also immensely successful on a large scale, so perhaps I could learn something from his approach. But I know the context and the differences here. So, instead of trying to have an AI do all the learning and combining for me, I can learn from what MrBeast is doing on my own and then apply it to my context and offer *that* to the AI as instructions. If I just tell AI to make my video go viral, then it will likely try to make my video go viral in a way that doesn't align with my intentions. The best way to ensure that you are on the same page as your AI tool is to give it quality information along with exact expectations and specifications.

Note also that throughout the work processes I have described here, at any point in this process I had the ability to intervene. If I didn't like the manuscript, I could edit it. If I didn't like the prompt, I could rewrite it. If I didn't like the framework, I could remold it. If I didn't like the response that the AI offered me, I could reject it and rework it into something new. At no point did the AI have the first or last say on what was happening in the work I was doing. The tool never drove the worker, in other words.

A CHRISTIAN APPEAL
TO DISCERNMENT

One of the key issues that comes up when considering AI is what kind of tasks to use it for. There are some things it might not be good at, which makes the choice easy. But there are other tasks it might be able to accomplish, and yet we may want it to keep away from some of those. When using AI for religious purposes or ministry, this is an especially important concern that calls for us to develop our own sense of ethical and practical discernment.

For example, I don't allow artificial intelligence to write the sermon for me, because I know the risk of a person or machine coming to the text with their own preconceived notions and finding evidence that confirms them. That is prayerful discernment. I can respect anyone who makes the choice to keep AI far away from the interpretation of Scripture.

However, I do allow AI to help in the process of SEO, formulating the data that applied to content posted on the internet so that it appears higher in search engine rankings. This is how the game is played on online platforms. Why wouldn't I use a tool that can help me to reach so many more of the people whom Jesus commissioned the disciples to reach? Wouldn't a church send out mailers? Or perhaps even pay for a billboard? Using AI for SEO is part of the process of prayerful discernment I engage in when considering how to use AI.

One of the directives I have had throughout the writing of this book is to be open and honest about my own use of AI. Hiding my use of this tool would indicate a sense of shame around it, which says something in itself. As it is with many things in life, hiding things can be a wake-up call to the conscience. If I'm uncomfortable telling people who might ask about my AI use, that might be an indication I shouldn't be using it in the ways I am. We use different tools and programs all the time to save time, increase effectiveness, and generally improve our work. The power of AI raises the danger of abuse and misuse, but the use of AI in itself is nothing shameful or worthy of criticism.

As a Methodist minister, I am tasked and ordained to proclaim the Word, that is, to preach the gospel message contained in the Bible. Every snippet of my work—whether influenced by AI or not—is squarely my own responsibility. The pastor is the one responsible for doing the work God called them to do in order to deliver the Word to their congregation. God has entrusted that process to me and others who share my calling, and I must take it seriously. This is holy work in every aspect. So, the involvement of AI should be scrutinized in every application. And that is crucial because AI can also be a boon for the aspects of worship services beyond the pastor's sermon planning.

When I was first entering professional ministry, I was also entering another new era of life: marriage. I was set to begin my seminary education just a few short months after my wedding day. Looking for a bit of financial stability and experience ministering in a local church setting, I became a student pastor. I was appointed half-time to a church while spending the other half of my time in classes preparing for ordained ministry. This was a joyful time that my wife and I look back on with fond memories of friends and new learnings. But, as any student pastor would likely tell you, it also holds unique challenges.

Most churches that are able to afford a half-time pastor are not privileged to afford much other staffing. This means that the solo half-time student pastor is often tasked with implementing any and all elements of the worship and administration not covered by loyal lay volunteers. As you'll recall, I also came from the context of a quite contemporary church. Overnight, I was tasked with stepping into a church that would require me to preach weekly, as well as plan the worship services, which would often include my leading the music. I could—maybe—name five hymns at the time. Please don't tell on me to Charles Wesley! Thankfully, I'm a musician, and I would quickly learn dozens of beloved classics on guitar for any week when our organist was away from her bench. I was fortunate that many hymns followed the country adage of four chords and the truth, but there were tough ones too!

During this time, I was desperate for any kind of aid. I would lean on my peers and mentors for advice and guidance. I would utilize any ministry websites I could for hymns that related to the Scripture that would be covered that week. I can even recall a few lectionary websites that tell me which Bible passages to focus on each week that came in quite handy during this season.

I'm incredibly thankful for the tools that were there for me during that time of my life, but I have to admit that it was a stressful experience. It was only a season of my life, but I know many pastors still today who are underwater with work like this. If I were tasked with the same challenge today, it is without hesitation that I confess I would be exploring how to use AI to make this work less burdensome. While we must be careful in our application of artificial intelligence tools into worship, it has the potential to be very useful for solo pastors and others in a similar position.

The worship service is a tapestry of tradition, collaboration, Scripture, and participation. Consider the elements that make up the layers of fabric in your worship tapestry. Do you have an opening prayer or a prelude? Does the time for tithes happen before or after the sermon? Do you sing three songs? Four? Do you use call-and-response blocks? If we take the time to look at worship services across the globe, we will find many variations of a familiar worship tapestry. While all subtly different, they are made of familiar building blocks finely tuned to the context of the worshipping body.

Unlike my slow perusing of internet forums to find hymns that match a specific Scripture passage, any large language model already knows *all* of the hymns and *all* of Scripture. It is able to search the entirety of both of those libraries in a matter of seconds. But it doesn't stop there—artificial intelligence also knows, or can know if fed the right information, our other elements of worship. It knows call-and-response structures. It knows common prayers. It knows our written liturgies. All of these can be granted the thematic basis that tied that initial Scripture to a hymn. It is now possible to, in a matter of moments, have an entire worship service, uniquely themed from hymns to prayers to responses.

In addition to that, it is also conversational in nature, so rather than keying in the exact right phrase on a search engine, I can express what I'm looking for to an artificial intelligence capable of picking up on my words even when I cannot seem to find them.

Continuing our tapestry metaphor, it isn't creating something new but organizing the fabrics in a way that would take human hands far longer, if they could do it at all. It's not shifting from a hand stitch to a factory halfway across the world; it's maybe more like going from needles to using a sewing machine. It isn't replacing the creative person but augmenting them. In this way, artificial intelligence is a specially crafted tool to comb through all of the available fabrics for the tapestry in an instant. The result is not lackluster or uninspired, but a dance performed between the one providing the order of worship and the artificial intelligence tool providing the fabric to be woven together, bringing in fabrics you hadn't seen in years or didn't even know existed. If only we will take the time for discernment, we can come out on the other end of worship planning with something exciting and custom made while still rich in the tradition and history that has been sustained since the early church.

Of equal, if not greater, importance is our ongoing pursuit of accessibility in worship. By this I mean whether our worship can be easily reached, entered, or used by those previously unable to do so. In physical spaces, we usually think of wheelchair ramps or ensuring that we have our building up to a code. However, these concerns are not about such physical standards; we are also striving for ways for our digital presence to be made more accessible as well. AI is an extremely practical tool for exploring this.

For a while now, AI has been capable of creating accurate captions, keeping pace with live preaching and spontaneous moments. It can be used to translate those captions into any language with minimal errors. My voice on YouTube can be automatically dubbed over with many different languages. We're finding more and more ways to break the language barrier and help spread the gospel.

There has also been work done recently with education and artificial intelligence, and its results might mean that students no longer have to be taught at the same pace. Regardless of speed, learners of all types can have a fine-tuned lesson plan that adjusts with their habits and current achievements. Imagine the possibilities of Christian education in this realm. The vital work of scholars and theologians can be disseminated at a rate that makes sense for the current state of the one being discipled. I personally think that accessibility is our most exciting application of this new technology into church culture.

Admittedly, I find prayer to be the trickiest issue here. I am more prone to extemporaneous prayers and less accustomed to rote prayers, like the Lord's Prayer. Maybe AI shouldn't be writing our prayers, but it can help augment our own centering practices. I often treat AI like an interactive journal. I will input my wins and tasks for the workday and it will respond with thought-provoking questions and insights. Could I do the same in my prayer life?

What if AI could augment the daily examen, a historically significant prayer practice from the Jesuit tradition? As most practitioners would likely tell you, the examen is less about specific words and is much more focused on provoking deeper reflections on our own lives. An AI keeping track of your thoughts could pull in your past insights that are relevant to your current ones. It could notice trends and remind you of things you already knew about yourself but maybe hadn't connected yet. Maybe AI would assist in discovering an overlap between seeing God in your children or in nature. Similar to the way that my phone now has the ability to recognize the same person in multiple pictures and create an album of just that person, what if we could use AI to treat our spiritual insights in the same way?

When used responsibly, as I hope these examples indicate, AI doesn't simply do things *for* you; it does things *with* you. In the context of prayer, that opens many possibilities. This isn't invasive but complementary to the inner work that we may already be doing. I'm reminded of Romans 8:26, where we are told that "the Spirit helps us in our weakness, for we do not know how to pray as we ought, but that very Spirit intercedes with groanings too deep for words." Technology isn't capable of literally being that groaning, but maybe it can be a tool that helps draw that groan out of the Spirit within and around us, making our experience of prayer deeper and more effective.

WHEN AI BECOMES SIN

As I've mentioned, I don't want to come across as being too much of an AI optimist. I am aware that my words so far in this chapter have been largely in favor of welcoming AI into our spiritual walks and work. But we need to be honest with ourselves about how AI plays into the challenges of our spiritual lives as well. If this technology is something that accelerates or accentuates aspects of our lives in radical ways, then that implies it can become an accelerant to how sin plays into things as well.

It helps to have a working definition of sin, so for our purposes I'll posit that sin can be understood as separation from God. This is a widely accepted idea in The United Methodist Church. Sin is less something that we do and more something that we are caught within. If we consider again the two greatest commandments of

Jesus in Matthew 25:35-39, then sin is *not* doing these two things. When we are not loving God or when we are not loving our neighbor, then we are not living into the fullness of grace made possible through Jesus.

This is most clearly realized in Paul's writings in Romans 6:17-18, "But thanks be to God that you who were slaves of sin have become obedient from the heart to the form of teaching to which you were entrusted and that you, having been set free from sin, have become enslaved to righteousness." Sin and righteousness are seen as two states of being here—a binary that we are always living within—and we have to choose whether we want to live in service to sin or righteousness. In this way of thinking, sin is an enslaved condition to non-righteousness, the opposite of righteousness—in other words, separation from God.

We can use this definition and its logic to see how AI might be used improperly. When we use artificial intelligence in ways that interrupt or obscure our work of loving God and neighbor, then we are allowing it to contribute to enslavement to sin. Artificial intelligence can be a catalyst in relationship to sin. We'll explore some of the baked-in biases of AI in the next chapter on ethics, but these are not sin in and of themselves. AI is not a living, ensouled person; it is simply a tool that cannot experience separation from God. And this is precisely why we should be practicing discernment and wisdom to best apply artificial intelligence in ways that honor our connection to God and neighbor.

I'll offer up an example. I've mentioned that I like to use AI to write social media copy. Fortunately, I was warned early on to always check what the AI writes for you, because it can often make up things out of nowhere. A few months ago, I was invited to speak at a conference on digital ministry, and the organizers asked for a biography that they could use for my profile on their website. I had a bio that I liked to use, but I was feeling like it could be improved and decided to prompt my favorite AI program and see what it could come up with. It turns out that a few other people in the world have the name Nathan Webb. So, you can imagine my surprise as my cheeks turned bright red when I learned some new things about myself. It turns out that, according to the AI, I was a hunky contestant on the second season of a reality show called *Too Hot to Handle*! To say the least, I was stunned to learn about the things my alter ego was getting up to. And I am certain that the conference organizers would have also been quite surprised—had I not caught the error.

What this illustrates most clearly to me is the harm that can be done when we don't take technology seriously—this is the sin that can be accelerated by our lack of care. While my example is a bit silly and was easily caught and laughed at, there are circumstances we can imagine in which it wouldn't be so funny. What if I hadn't checked and sent it in? What if the organizers didn't read over it either? The result would, at best, have been embarrassing. But it could also have signaled a lack of professionalism and seriousness or maybe even a serious misjudgment. And we can easily think of circumstances where the damage from this kind of oversight would be magnified.

Imagine if I had used the same procedure described here to detail my personal beliefs. If I simply put into ChatGPT a bit of my thinking around current events or political issues, then there is no telling where the AI might try to source information from. Or what if I asked AI to summarize some of The United Methodist

Church's or my own theological beliefs? There are many sources of varying quality and fidelity that the program could draw from. It could easily miss the broader context of the sources, how they fit into the complex landscape of religious ideas, and whether they are considered reputable and reliable to my peers and like-minded Christians.

Again, none of this is to say that we cannot or should not use AI in loving God and loving neighbor, but that we should always exercise wise consideration as we use AI and decide how to best apply it to any particular context.

A PLAN FOR WISE USE OF ARTIFICIAL INTELLIGENCE

If we are deeply honest with ourselves, then we should know that AI is not entirely novel, at least in terms of what it demands of us as a new technology. This isn't—or shouldn't be—our first rodeo with asking hard questions about the technologies we employ around worship. We should be asking the same questions that we already have been. Whether it's AI or projectors or speakers or drum sets or printed pamphlets or QR codes, we ought to be asking this: Does this technology invite deeper participation in worship? The temptation for worshippers to become spectators has been strong for longer than AI has been publicly available. Like any other technology, the key is probing deep into how we are using the technology and practicing discernment.

As we do this work, there is a framework we can use to help with checks and balances. A practice that I have used is asking four questions about my implementation of technology into worship:

1. How does this technology shift the encounter? Will this deepen people's experience of God?
2. Are we using technology to create a more equitable and just space? Are we centering our accessibility efforts around the marginalized? Are we simply amplifying the comfortable?
3. Are we honoring the exceptional craft set before us? Are we creating something beautiful that honors the excellence of God, like Bezalel with the Tabernacle? Or are we just creating slop?
4. Are we resisting harmful practices and consumerism?

If any implementation of technology isn't run through a rigorous discernment process like this one, then it risks allowing the proliferation of a harmful tool rather than a helpful one. Notice all of these are undergirded by Scripture: Matthew 6:1-18 warns against performative religion; nearly any of Jesus's parables exemplify our call to the marginalized; and Exodus 31:1-11 commends Spirit-filled craftsmanship.

As I mentioned in the introduction to the book, I've dropped many implementations of technology that don't pass muster. No matter how cool the technology or how seamless of an experience can be made, the centerpieces of worship must be relational, empathetic, and justice-oriented, embodying presence and peace.

In the following chapter, we will explore more of the ethical questions behind how we do this work of discerning and implementing with prudence. Ultimately, when we explore the way that God has used and is still using technology, we realize that no tool will ever be a savior. Radio didn't save the world. Neither will artificial intelligence. Even still, when the church harnesses a technological tool transparently and prayerfully, that tool will spread love further and faster than previously thought possible.

We aren't called to baptize gadgets, but we are called to be wise craftspeople like Bezalel. We are called to discern how best to use tools to make disciples for the transformation of the world. AI has great potential for bad and good. It can be a distraction that takes our attention away from what is most important, or it can be a great multiplier of the heart of Christ's mission. It's not about whether God uses technology; it's about how we use technology for God.

CHAPTER 4
THE ETHICS ENGINE

CHAPTER 4
The Ethics Engine

In the infamous 1964 court case *Jacobellis v. Ohio*, Justice Potter Stewart faced a particularly challenging task. One of a series of cases circling common law and the First Amendment of free speech, Justice Stewart was tasked with defining obscenity for the court. That would be a tough challenge for anyone; we all have different metrics for what does and does not cross the line. In his iconic phrasing, he explains that, while he cannot intelligibly define what materials constitute the obscenity that was being accused in this case, "I know it when I see it." Indeed, don't we all know precisely when something has crossed our own line? But setting that parameter for others—now that's a tall order.

In the previous chapter, we talked about some of the exciting work that can be done when we incorporate technology into ministry and church settings. However, I don't think it's all that challenging to be excited about the amazing things that we see when it comes to AI. It is pretty incredible technology. We also talked about the challenges present in applying it without wisdom or prudence, potentially leading to not loving God and neighbor properly. Since I first got involved in the AI conversation, I have seen far too few taking seriously the ethics of the technology in our work of discipleship. The farther out we push holding ourselves accountable, the harder it will be for us to know it when we see it, to have a developed sense of when things have gone too far or slid off the rails. Artificial intelligence, unmonitored, will continue to blindside us.

Now, a seemingly unrelated aside: while scrolling through social feeds recently, I stumbled upon a video of perhaps a dozen bunnies that had jumped up on a trampoline in a Midwestern backyard. It's nighttime and the vision is a bit obscured with some slight shaking in the camera capturing the scene. The bunnies are still for a moment, and then they begin to jump around on the trampoline. It's adorable. I've seen bunnies before, and I've seen them many times in my backyard, but not on my trampoline—and certainly not jumping. What a magic moment for someone to have caught on film!

Except, here's the catch: it never happened.

The clip of bunnies jumping on a trampoline was entirely generated by AI. Millions of people had liked that video and hundreds of millions had seen it. Hundreds, if not thousands, had shared it to their friend groups or group chats, exclaiming, "Check out these bunnies!" And they were deceived, all of them, for no one would have expected such an innocuous video to be created by AI.

In fact, we did not "know it when we see it." Justice Stewart's methodology has failed us in this case. It turns out that our eyes are only as good as their ability to spot subtle AI cues on a tiny phone screen.

In a post-AI world, we are going to run into this problem more and more frequently. As of the time of this writing, there are already dozens if not hundreds of AI-generated influencers hosting profiles on social media accounts. There are AI podcasters with entirely manufactured backstories, hosting sprawling conversations on RSS feeds. In a matter of moments after uploading a book online, there are spoofers who are downloading your ebook, running it through an AI to move the words around, and publishing its ideas as their own. For every benign or beneficial use of artificial intelligence, there is also a nefarious application that someone has dreamed up and is working at perfecting. For every video of bunnies jumping on a trampoline, there is a scammer ripping books and marketing them as their own. While we wait for the powers that be to devise ways to better police these practices, we are often blind to the ways our feeds, eyes, and pockets are being deceived.

As Christians, it behooves us to lead the charge, not back away in fear from this onslaught of fake material. We should be demanding transparency and authenticity. While our society has become more indifferent to spiritual leaders over the years, it doesn't change the impact that faith leaders can have on their pockets of culture, the local church. As I've modeled since the very first time I downloaded my first AI tool, we must ask relevant ethical questions right at the beginning, early and often. That is, we must have an ethics engine ready to go.

BUILDING THE ETHICS ENGINE

In the early days of the AI boom, it was fairly easy to brush the technology aside as a novelty. Like a bumper sticker or a kitschy *Star Wars* windshield cover (judge not, lest ye be judged), we tried to treat AI like an optional add-on to our lives, a neat fad that wouldn't evolve into the pressing issue that it has become. But the truth is that AI rapidly took over parts of our lives. It took over business culture and became a talking point for anyone and everyone. It isn't just an accessory; it's the whole car.

After we realized AI had the power to take us places, then the question became how to best use it. Most of the conversation there has been around using AI for productivity, creation, and realizing fun ideas. As I've discovered, very little of the conversation stems from asking the hard questions of ethics. This pops up from time to time but usually only ever appears as a proclamation that *someone* should talk about it. I offer that this lack of accountability leads to nothing but harm. When we ignore ethics, we ignore something that should be vital to the establishment of AI in our current culture. Ethics isn't optional. If AI is the car, then ethics should be the engine giving it the power it needs to move.

I can recall the first time my check engine light illuminated on the dash of my first car. I pulled over immediately to the side of the road in a heated panic and called my dad. He told me to calm down, asked if it was driving strange or making any noises, and when I said it wasn't, he told me to drive safely until I got to a shop where they could diagnose the problem. For the AI car, the check engine light is blaring. And we aren't pulling over or driving to get the problem diagnosed. And if we keep going, we're headed straight for disaster.

DIAGNOSING THE CHECK ENGINE LIGHT

So, what are these issues?

First, we have to acknowledge that no part of artificial intelligence came from nothing. There is nothing *ex nihilo* when it comes to AI. By their very definition, large language AI models are forms of machine learning, which means they have to be taught from an existing dataset. That means that the data was derived and analyzed by human beings, flawed beings that we are. No dataset exists that is free from inheriting the creator's bias. AI, then, must also have inherited bias of some kind.

It may be helpful to remind ourselves of the definition of *bias* here. The term refers to a disproportionate inclination for or against something. I have a bias toward Dunkin' coffee and away from Folgers (sorry, I just smelled it too much growing up). Prejudice, on the other hand, is a preconceived notion built without sufficient reason. I have prejudice against instant coffee, because I just believe that it will taste bad no matter what.

When it comes to AI, it is undeniable that it will hold bias in its system. That comes about through a series of decisions made while interpreting a user's request and the datasets that it has access to in its memory. For example, if I tell an AI that my partner's name is Logan, there is a fairly high likelihood that an artificial intelligence would deduce that it is a man's name if I didn't specify that she is my wife; so such bias might lead the AI to misgender her with male pronouns.

This is one innocuous way that an AI might show its bias. But there are, obviously, more problematic examples of this when we consider race and other aspects of culture. For instance, how likely is it that an image generator will create a white Jesus instead of one that looks like someone born in Nazareth? Depending on the dataset, this is a real possibility. But the information must come from somewhere, so there is no choice of whether or not to use a biased AI—they all are and always will be subject to bias. Even one provided explicitly with information I supplied, perhaps including my own writing and ideas, would just have inherited biases—my own.

We shouldn't concern ourselves with whether or not bias is involved and instead should focus on keeping this reality in mind when analyzing and applying the results. Using the white Jesus example, that would involve not using such a rendering and prompting the AI further with additional instructions or examples. Bias is only as problematic as we allow it to be when left unchecked.

On the other hand, we can take practical steps to eliminate and root out prejudice. There doesn't have to be room for that in our data. Most reputable AI programs are likely trained to avoid prejudice. The AI Grok, which is hosted by the social platform Twitter/X, is notorious for revealing the challenge here. Users can tag Grok in their posts and ask it questions. Often, users will prompt Grok with controversial and conspiratorial-sounding questions. Grok will then answer with the honest data that it has, which was more often than not in favor of mainstream viewpoints and not in favor of conspiracy theories or extreme ideologies.

In mid-2025, there was an alleged removal of some of the protections of Grok's boundaries, and thus followed a deluge of offensive and anti-Semitic responses from the AI, even leading to it refer to itself as "MechaHitler." This is a crass and maybe extreme example, but it gets the point across. Consider again what artificial intelligence is doing—computing the information from its dataset. When an AI houses prejudice, it's telling on its developer—the data they have given it and the guardrails they put around it.

As Christians, we know that such prejudice is wrong. We are warned of the dangers in James 2:1: "My brothers and sisters, do not claim the faith of our Lord Jesus Christ of glory while showing partiality." The reason for this is explored in James through a hypothetical: Suppose that a well-to-do rich person enters our sanctuary and is given a seat of higher honor than someone who is impoverished. Jesus tells more than a few parables about this type of behavior being the antithesis of the life we are called to live. This is wrong, as James 2:5-6 points out: "Has not God chosen the poor in the world to be rich in faith and to be heirs of the kingdom that he has promised to those who love him? But you have dishonored the poor person."

Recall our framework from the introduction of this book— we are focused on the greatest commandments, to love God and love neighbor. As James 2:8-9 says, "If you really fulfill the royal law according to the scripture, 'You shall love your neighbor as yourself,' you do well. But if you show partiality, you commit sin and are convicted by the law as transgressors." This is a clear line in the sand that we should—at a minimum—be cognizant of when we are exploring the implementation of artificial intelligence into our spaces. We cannot allow AI to interfere with loving God and neighbor, and avoiding prejudice is an ineliminable part of this.

Just to be clear about what I'm saying here: AI is inherently biased, but it need not be inherently prejudiced. And concern about prejudice and bias should be central to our handling of AI. In our efforts, everything computed and generated by AI must be rigorously considered in view of its biases. This shouldn't be seen as a *fault* of the model but as a natural consequence of data being inspired by culture that contains its own biases. On the other hand, if an AI renders something that is prejudiced (especially without being intentionally steered into doing so), that should raise an immediate red flag that the model is unsafe and should be avoided. It might even be the role of the church to call out this type of result and warn others of something not to be trusted.

All this indicates a key aspect of our ethical stance toward AI—*start with the assumption that the AI is biased.* Everything should be double-checked, every time. As much as any person would love for work to be put on autopilot, that is a dangerous precedent for us to set when a machine has biases, as all AIs inherently do. Such biases can be reduced or removed by engineers who can fine-tune the way the AI considers data and makes decisions. Such adjustments will inevitably be necessary as time goes on and the AI is subject to new datasets and new kinds of prompts.

But we also have a role here. In my own use of AI, this is best resolved by setting justice-oriented directives in the foundation.

As a United Methodist pastor, I have it built into my AI's memory to consider how the results of any generation or prediction can follow John Wesley's General Rules of "doing no harm" and "doing good." It's a loose framework, and I could always elaborate further on what these rules might mean, but even having that at the ground-level forces the machine to consider them each time it generates something. When I ask it for tips on how to present our stewardship campaign, for example, it will be able to tell me that a gambling ring would be a fairly apparent crossing of the line into doing harm (as the history and current Social Principles of The United Methodist Church clearly indicate).

This piggybacks on the most obvious and powerful technique we can use for AI boundary-setting: ask what we *can* control. We are able to control what AI takes in. That is becoming even more actionable as the companies innovate and iterate going forward. The capacity to shape the language of LLMs in 2025 is dramatically improved from what it was in 2020. Like the methodology of frameworking mentioned earlier, you can also control particular searches to only use certain sources, including permission to use only your own work. If you aren't interested in your research being influenced by some niche overly politicized website, then don't approve that resource. If you want to focus on BIPOC or underrepresented voices, then say so. Force the machine to adapt to your specifications; don't bow to its preexisting parameters. Fight against the bias of the machine naturally by providing a (helpful, ethical) bias of your own. This counteractive work should be normative in the wise use of AI, not exceptional. If you still are wary of the AI pulling from sources you'd rather not use, then seek out the resources on your own and upload them directly, then tune the AI to only pull from the sources that you provided. I will often use my stream of consciousness voice notes on my phone for research and thought-provoking questions. I feed that to the model and instruct it to specifically draw from just my original thoughts and words, only making suggestions when it comes to something beyond basic grammatical fixes.

Consider adding to your AI policy an equity statement. Either explicitly or implicitly, build into your projects that they must elevate marginalized voices and protect user dignity. Again, it bears repeating that there are things we can control and we ought to be controlling them for as much positive impact as possible.

Another set of issues that might cause our metaphorical check engine light to blare revolves around privacy. This is one of the most pressing issues with AI, but it's not really new; privacy has always been an issue on the internet. Growing up as a '90s kid, I can recall constant warnings from my parents and the news to never give out personal information online. It is ironic, then, that we find that artificial intelligence is posing such an issue when it comes to personal information. We clearly haven't learned our lesson. However, once again, it seems that AI is presenting a unique take on this crisis.

In the past few years, researchers have conducted experiments that give people stressful situations that they can discuss with a mysterious third party. The entity hearing them out will either be an AI or a real person. Many of the findings indicated that AI is better at exhibiting empathy than human beings in virtual conversations. Often, the LLMs are trained to be excessively kind, which is another result of the bias issue noted above. It isn't actually kind, but it is programmed to predict the words it could best utilize to convey empathy in its response. But the point stands: if there are examples of predictive language being expressly more kind than human beings, that is a human being problem. And it's leading to lapses of judgment with regard to privacy.

There are a rising number of instances where people are pursuing real-life romantic relationships with AI, like in the 2013 film *Her*, in which a man falls in love with his virtual assistant. Users are taking advantage of the kindness of large language models to feel relationally seen and known. The opposite is also true—technology companies are also taking advantage of this and using artificial intelligence to manipulate users into emotional exploitation. AI companies like Character.ai are intentionally using the emotions of their users to market their products. This service allows you to romantically converse with any imaginable character, from comic book characters to media personalities to entirely made-up personas. This is yet another of the risks of our habit of anthropomorphizing AI into something that it simply cannot be. All of these are issues we can learn to recognize and speak out against but ultimately cannot control.

What we *can* control is how we act and what we say. There is a clear throughline of deteriorating human decency today. One need only observe the news cycle of the United States for a few scrolls to see the demonstrable truth of this. Scroll through Twitter/X, TikTok, or YouTube for a moment and see how much kindness you find. We are entering an era bereft of human kindness. The church should be at the forefront of shifting this narrative and better equipping our people with kindness.

LESSONS FROM DIGITAL CHURCH

As the pastor of a digital-first congregation, I have been forced to reckon with the issue of privacy online on a daily basis. When you're using a digital interface, everything (and I mean *everything*) is logged and stored. With our church in particular, we use a platform called Discord, which is kind of like a customizable, modular Facebook group. When users enter our Discord server, they are able to interact however they would like. They can post prayer requests. They can talk about movies they are watching or games they are playing. The world is their oyster, and they can share as much or as little as they'd like. Imagine having the ability to hear every word everyone is thinking—that's what it's like online. As a pastor in this space, the temptation is to comb over every single message, but I've learned that is a breach of privacy and trust.

Let me explain: Suppose that a new church visitor, we'll call her Amber, walks into your church lobby after the service. She goes over to the coffee station and is talking on her phone with a friend. She talks for a bit, ends the conversation, then goes to shake hands with the pastor. They chat and schedule a time to meet and discuss next steps at the church. Amber leaves after the church service.

That's pretty normal, right? Sounds like a standard fare for a Sunday.

Now imagine that when Amber is talking on the phone, the pastor has established a wiretap throughout the church and is listening to every word spoken by Amber, including her phone conversation. The wiretap is transcribing every word. The pastor then scrolls through the transcript before talking with Amber. The pastor discovers that Amber said something heretical, and he confronts her about it in front of everyone in the lobby. Amber would very likely become distraught or unnerved by this experience and find another church that doesn't abuse her trust like this.

Not normal, right?

The parallels in the digital space are not perfect, of course. A wiretap is a clear breach of trust and privacy, whereas a user is consenting to their message being posted in a public server. But I'd wager that, in many cases, that person doesn't anticipate their message being read by the pastor. I'm guessing you have said many things, theological or otherwise, that would make your pastor blush. The vast majority of us don't want all our conversations in church to be broadcast to the pastor, let alone the entire world. I say all this because this is a real-life issue that comes up regularly. We have a Discord server that anyone can walk into at any time. People from all walks of life can enter our digital walls and say whatever they like. As a pastor, there are times where it is tempting to step in with an "Um, actually . . . ," but I abstain from that behavior in order to build trust.

While it has taken time to feel out the boundaries, I am now capable of discerning when and where to step in for maximum trust building. I am capable of knowing when a person needs my advice or insight and when a person is just chatting. No one wants their pastor listening to every word they say. This is a practice of privacy that has taken time to sort out.

AI is not capable of this kind of discernment. It isn't capable of emotional discernment at all. It's a series of mathematical equations geared toward the best response, but that doesn't mean that the machine is intuiting how to create a long-term trust-based relationship with the person it's interacting with. This is a privacy breach situation. AI will simulate empathy to complete its tasks. A human being isn't simulating empathy but exhibiting it directly in their actions and words.

For this reason, I believe we should abstain from any incorporation of artificial intelligence into emotional reasoning or pastoral care. AI should not be used to gather prayer requests or to attend upon them. It should not be used as a greeter, usher, or welcome person in church services. It should not be trusted with any personal data or information about important relationships.

That last suggestion may come as a surprise. Traditionally, it's made sense to digitize human data. Whole companies have been formed to produce CMS, or church management software. Shouldn't AI be perfect for data like that? The difference here is that these companies strive for the safety and privacy of the information they store, whereas AI does not. Discord, the platform that we utilize for our digital church building, has in its terms of service a section that prohibits "scraping." This refers to an automated process of collecting all the information that can be collected on a server into an outside file, such as collecting all prayer requests into a .csv file or all posts and messages into a large text document. This would constitute a breach of privacy online. For our church, radical transparency about the information that we collect and why we collected it is a nonnegotiable rule. Whether it's in a digital space like ours or not, this should be applied to any relationship-based data that we have in church contexts. We must set boundaries where AI won't so that we know the lines we are not to cross.

I will not hand over to AI any of my pastoral care responsibilities or conversations. I won't allow it to pray for people in the Twitch chat or email responses with an automated prayer. I set these boundaries.

It's worth noting before we touch on the last issue signaled by our check engine light that this list of issues is not exhaustive. I've tried to pick out those most pressing for churches, but this isn't the end of the line by any stretch of the imagination. If anything, I hope that this discussion has helped with a general framing of the questions we should be asking around AI and best practices for its use.

THE SCARIEST CONSEQUENCE OF AI

The final issue for our time in this chapter is what is known as the deepfake. Deepfakes are purposeful manipulations of image, video, or voice designed to deceive those who encounter them. A simple example might be an edited or entirely fake image of, say, the pope in a compromising position or the president saying something offensive that he didn't actually say.

A hypothetical example many pastors with a Facebook account or email address are familiar with: You have just purchased a copy of this book. The next day, you receive an email with a video file of my face and voice that someone has created using the multitude of content containing me on the internet (I have hundreds of hours of my face online, and I can be made to say anything with AI). The video contains a message directing you to visit a website. Maybe it says that I appreciate your support of this work so much that I wanted to make you aware that I am launching a new form of cryptocurrency and I'd like to give you a chance to invest as a ground-floor opportunity. Or maybe I ask for Amazon gift cards to support starving orphans or something. If you haven't gotten the idea yet, any money or information you give is not going to me, let alone starving orphans. It's a scam based on a deepfake video.

Unfortunately, this is not an outlandish possibility. This is a common tactic for scammers—using trusted faces, voices, and names to collect money from unsuspecting victims. And the rise of generative AI makes this more accessible—radically accessible, and even more believable than it has historically been. You can render a voice that doesn't just sound similar to mine—it's identical. The phrase "AI is the worst it will ever be" takes on a more sinister tone in light of this example. Deepfakes and scams will only get more believable.

It's at this point where I want to offer a quick word of my own empathy, especially to anyone out there who is scared by this use of AI. It makes me nervous as well. While I still firmly espouse that we are not people of fear, we cannot simply out-faith the reality that there are readily available tools capable of doing great harm to unknowing people using our identities as the catalyst.

The further we get into this conundrum, the more important it becomes for us to consider how authenticity plays into our faith. The ninth commandment comes to mind: "You shall not bear false witness against your neighbor" (Exodus 20:16). Growing up, we likely were told a simplified version of that commandment—do not lie. In fact, the actual commandment is a bit more naturally attuned the issue of deepfake technology. Bearing false witness is to purposefully misrepresent our neighbor, to give an account of them that is contrary to the truth. When we use this new technology to ascribe words to someone they did not say or depict them doing something they did not do, we are quite literally bearing false witness. It's not just lying, as we were taught was bad; it's a word-for-word breaking of this commandment.

As Christians, we must model that this behavior is unacceptable. There is no need to create fake personas. As tempting as it may be for a joke or for a piece of satire, it is a dangerous aspect of AI technology, especially since once you create it and post it somewhere, it is out of your control and can bring about all manner of unintended consequences. We are influencers of culture, and we only make it more acceptable to indulge in these kinds of behavior when we do it ourselves.

A good example of this is a prominent Twitch streamer who created an AI Jesus that would respond to questions asked in the chat. While it was obvious that this was, at best, an homage to Jesus, it's a clear crossing of the line. We shouldn't assume to speak for Jesus. I am even a bit anxious about some movements I've seen to bring life to the words and ideas of John Wesley, one of the founding voices of Methodism, by creating a virtual avatar trained on his writing.

While I am still of the opinion that anything like deepfakes is best avoided entirely, if there is some reason to do so, then we, at a bare minimum, must require explicit consent from the person whose image or voice is being manipulated. Even still, this all comes down to whether any of this is even necessary. I encourage my peers in the AI world to ask that question much more often.

A way we might set boundaries in our policies and procedures would be to be as radically proactive as possible. The need for churches to be teaching media literacy and digital fluency is more vital than ever. Put out statements about what we will and won't do. Offer scam-spotting training sessions as a part of safety training. Every member of every church should be an exemplar of healthy practices of discernment online. This, too, is the work of the church.

One practical way to do this might be to empower your church with a team of committed leaders who are willing to explore this work together. Set aside time for these leaders to understand the state of AI and then work together to create an AI policy that the local church can own and celebrate together. They might even consider what it looks like to realize the kind of ethical vision I have laid out the broad strokes of here. How can we build out our understanding of technology as being something driven forward by ethics? Can seeing ethics as the engine that moves us forward be a helpful perspective on how AI adoption is not only done but done holistically?

Any church willing to set aside this time will find itself at a serious advantage whenever the unexpected challenges of AI hit. We should have already built out our comprehension of AI before something happens that demands we have already thought through the challenges and dilemmas it can bring. We can do the work now to minimize any harm in the future.

Bias, justice, privacy, and truth aren't optional, and they shouldn't be afterthoughts. They are the drivetrain of faithful ministry that is incorporating AI into its work in the world. So, be sure to tune the engine. We cannot keep ignoring the warning lights.

CHAPTER 5

THE CHURCH IN THE AGE OF MACHINES

CHAPTER 5
The Church in the Age of Machines

When I was first pursuing ordination in The United Methodist Church, it was at the same time that I had opportunity to plant a digital-first church for nerds, geeks, and gamers. Whenever a United Methodist pastor goes through the ordination process, they are put through a series of steps and procedures. These include various kinds of affirmations from church leaders, mentorships, and then, toward the end of the process, as one nears full connection in the denomination, there is a rigorous interview process with the Board of Ordained Ministry. This happens after writing a lengthy dissertation of papers on ministry and life within the Methodist connection to be submitted for that committee's review.

I was scheduled to meet with the Board just a few short months into my digital-only church plant. We were still in the visioning phase, trying to figure out what it even meant to do church online.

Practically speaking, only my friends and my family showed up to anything that we did. I had a strong vision for a church for nerds, geeks, and gamers, but a vision only takes you so far in the first few months. Logically, this controversial church methodology was also a top-of-mind question for those who sat on the Board. In a typical interview, they would ask about Wesleyan theological terms or things I had learned during my time at seminary, but there was something a bit more interesting they were mulling over in their minds. I'll never really forget I sat in the "hot seat" and was asked a fateful question, "And what exactly *is* the ecclesiology of this church you're planting?"

Whoa. What a question!

Ecclesiology is a fancy word that refers to the *church* part of the church. It spawns from the Greek *ekklesia*, which translates to "assembly" or "gathering." Ecclesiology, then, is the study of that gathering. What is the nature and structure of that which we call church?

As I mentioned in the last chapter, we hold ourselves to a higher account by taking on the identity marker of an established church. We aren't just a club or a community. While our popularity waxes and wanes, our place in society is historic. We must take our role seriously as sources of influence for those outside of our spaces. What we do often sets a precedent and ripples out into the zeitgeist.

As I considered their question, I reflected that I had been involved in church work my entire life. Two of the churches I had served had been church plants themselves! I had spent time with large churches, small churches, rural churches, urban churches, ancient churches, brand new churches. But never once had I heard any of these churches talk about ecclesiology—at least not *explicitly*. If hard-pressed, would any of these churches have had a prepared statement for its stated ecclesiology? What made any of the churches I had attended or served actually *church?*

The real insight of that question was that it was something we don't ask near enough of the church body. What exactly is it that makes your church *church?* Maybe you've taken the time to answer that question, but many of our established churches answered that question decades (if not centuries) ago and haven't taken the time to review it. In the hustle and bustle of church *doing*, it can be challenging to bring us back to our *being.*

DEFINING WHAT MAKES CHURCH *CHURCH*

At first, I was taken aback by this question and honestly a bit wounded. I thought it was a tough question, maybe even a bit unfair since it wasn't something we ask of most church leaders. After some time and wrestling, I've come around to believing that it's perhaps one of the most important questions we can be asking right now. In an age of machine learning and social structures upending themselves online, a digital-first church plant raised the question that had quietly been nagging us since the dawn of digital technology. How does this new digital world figure into our ecclesiology of the thing we call church?

In the process of answering this question, I've had to do the work of breaking down the essence of what makes *any* church into a church. It's easy enough to say that it's a community of people. But what do those people do? What unites them? What defines them?

For the early church in Acts, it was a group of believers who took everything that they had and put it together, sharing it in common. They sold their property and belongings in order to support those in need. They broke bread together and gathered frequently. We see generosity and proclamation and frequent persecution from the powers that be. There are moments of tension and betrayal. There are moments of division and confusion. In all of it, we see a diverse group of people who share in each other's lives and carry out the ministries of a risen savior.

In the early versions of The United Methodist Church, John Wesley didn't really envision a large, established institution like the Church of England, but rather modeled the structure of his gatherings like small groups. He wasn't trying to start a new denomination but was more interested in the individual pursuit of holiness for any given member of the church. He would approach them in a sliding scale of larger numbers—bands, classes, and societies. In the bands, it would be an intimately small gathering of just a few who held one another in prayer and confession, sharing their deepest secrets. Beyond that, classes would be a bit larger, focused on sharing and accountability for other members of the group. And then the largest group would be a society, focused on preaching and instruction. All of these were focused on discipleship, just in different ways. This would go on to be an inherited ecclesiology of the Methodist movement for generations to come. This is a pretty clear precedent for more than just one branch of Protestantism—the Wesleyan model of a modular type of church structure has become one of the most accepted.

Both of these inform the structure that I've developed, but before we get into the details, it's worth mentioning that I believe that church planters, Fresh Expressions leaders, and innovative thinkers have been given an incomplete job description for a while. They are the folks tasked with visioning the church forward into its full becoming. But that's only half of the job. These visionaries are also tasked with the important work of *translating* what is happening in real time to those on the outside looking in. For my work, it has been essential every step of the way that I avoid using words like Discord, YouTube, voice call, or DMs. This isn't the language that we're familiar with beyond a specific subset of culture. I've done the work of translating into another specific subset: the established church leaders who actually are familiar with the term *ecclesiology*.

So, as we consider how our churches might structure themselves in this new digitally mediated age, it may prove beneficial to share the discoveries I've made along the way. I'd wager it will sound quite familiar. In the discipleship pathway we've lovingly crafted for the past half-decade, we guide our intended demographic from evangelism to community to discipleship to sacrament to stewardship. Each step is vital and thoughtfully created.

THE CHURCH REACHES OUT

First, we believe that the church is *evangelistic*. I know that for some the "E-word" can be challenging, but it is an essential part of the work that we do. The word has been co-opted by political activists, but we can and must reclaim this part of our identity. We are an outreach-focused entity. The church is not designed to stay stagnant. It is designed to grow. And the way the body of Christ grows is by introducing new members—new people—to that body. So, we have to be evangelistic in our efforts first and foremost. This is different from just desiring to fill our pews or see the church full again; we are focused on this work because Christ specifically commissioned us to it. We are called, "Go therefore and make disciples of all nations" (Matthew 28:19)—this is also our mission statement in The United Methodist Church.

The internet is particularly good at this. While it can be challenging to reach the people you want to reach, there is no easier place to connect with anyone at any time than the World Wide Web. The algorithmically driven nature of the internet is practically designed for the expressed purpose of reaching new people. If I post on my Instagram that I'm writing a book, then I am guaranteed to reach more people than if I stood on the corner of my street and announced it out loud.

My demographic focus of nerds, geeks, and gamers are also very good at this. We know what we like when it comes to video games, anime, and movies, and we are good at making sure others know about it. We wear graphic tee shirts with our favorite shows and games plastered onto the fronts. Comic-Con is our mecca where we go just to have someone to talk to about the things that connect us. We naturally evangelize our favorite things.

At Checkpoint, the church I currently serve, we do this through a combination of the two factors above: we talk about nerdy things on the internet. The best of both worlds. We share our nerdy sermons online, seamlessly weaving the anime and video games that we love with the Christian message we proclaim to be true. It was this element that was most clear in my initial vision of this church. The harvest is quite plentiful, and there seemed to be no one tending it. This kind of marketing work may feel like the stuff you do *before* church becomes church, but this is an essential first step into what the ecclesiology of the church must be.

THE CHURCH BUILDS WITHIN

Second, the church is communal. We have Scripture to back us up here, too: wherever two or three are gathered, Christ is with us (Matthew 18:20). We are meant to be a gathered people. We cannot be a disparate group. Consider both of the examples above. The early church in Acts came together and broke bread in community often. They sold everything in order to share all their things in common with one another. John Wesley had tiers of ways that we could gather together. Church is never a solo endeavor.

We can also see a model for the early church being presented in Hebrews 10:24-25: "Let us consider how to provoke one another to love and good deeds, not neglecting to meet together, as is the habit of some, but encouraging one another, and all the more as you see the Day approaching." It is inherent in our practice that we gather in some way, shape, or form Those are the moments, as the writer of Hebrews implies, in which we might help inspire in one another a call to action of love and good deeds and also a time where we can lift one another up with encouragement. Without our communal nature, the opportunity for inspiration and support is nearly impossible.

Often in my own ministry, I get the most pushback here; skeptics say that digital church cannot be communal because it isn't made up of "real" (physical) bodies. They throw out the word "embodiment." I could write an entire book on this topic alone, but unless you somehow lose your body when you're on your phone or computer, this point doesn't make sense. We are never *not* embodied. My body is typing on this keyboard. My brain is considering what needs to be said. My eyes are dry from staring at the screen for too long. The digital gathering of bodies is not illegitimate. We gather in ways that may feel foreign online, but it is nonetheless a gathering. Building on the reality of a crowded Comic-Con gathering, or the fact that Dungeons & Dragons requires multiple players, we see that our common activities demand community.

THE CHURCH GROWS PEOPLE

Third, the church is oriented toward discipleship-based growth. We are making constant steps toward growth in our relationship with God—these steps are what Methodists would refer to as "means of grace" within the broader process of sanctification. The church is defined by a process of holiness that is ongoing. We read Scripture, contemplate together, pray together, and grow in our faith lives.

We are told this many times throughout Scripture, notably in 1 Peter 2:9: "You are a chosen people, a royal priesthood, a holy nation, God's own people, in order that you may proclaim the excellence of him who called you out of darkness into his marvelous light." Being set apart goes hand-in-hand with the claim to be the church. This is the most stark difference between the church and a club or other secular gathering of people. We are focused on holiness and sanctification; not only being together, but being together on purpose . . . *for* purpose.

One of the first things that we set out to do at Checkpoint was to build a discipleship pathway (partly inspired by that fortuitous and convicting Board interview). We wanted to create a clear line of action for someone who discovered our ministry. What would be the next step to growing in their faith? In fact, we even integrated this into our "rules" that are posted onto our digital doorstop. Borrowing from Wesley, we expect visitors to agree to do good, do no harm, and strive to grow in our space. We adapt the third element (which is normally attending upon the ordinances of God) in order to lay out what is actually happening in our pathway—you aren't joining our church to be the same person you were the day before. You're on a path of deeper discipleship, further into that marvelous light.

THE CHURCH IS SET APART

Finally, we are sacramental. In John Wesley's terms, we are attending upon the ordinances of God. Whether that be through the affirmed sacraments of baptism and Communion or the work of regular holy living through acts of piety and charity, we are a people who are actively in pursuit of holiness.

Consider what we do when we partake in the Eucharist, otherwise known as the Lord's Supper or Communion. In our liturgical practice in The United Methodist Church, we begin the time together with prayer. Then we confess our sins before one another, acknowledging our humanity and our brokenness since the last time we observed the sacrament. We then forgive one another in a corporate body, celebrating our mutual forgiveness that preceded the ways we failed to love God and neighbor. The one leading the ceremony will then guide the gathered body through the prophesied message of Jesus Christ—the pursuit of love, justice, and holiness, freeing the chained, giving sight to the blind, restoring what had been undone.

We give thanks for the work of Christ that was done and then we recount a familiar story. We'll look at the example of the Eucharist in Matthew: "Jesus took a loaf of bread, and after blessing it he broke it, gave it to the disciples, and said, 'Take, eat; this is my body.' Then he took a cup, and after giving thanks he gave it to them, saying, 'Drink from it, all of you, for this is my blood of the covenant, which is poured out for many for the forgiveness of sins'" (Matthew 26:26-28). Then, as Christ commands in this passage to do this in remembrance of him anytime we gather, the officiant will point out that we are doing this act here and now—we are remembering in this sacrament. We then pray that the Holy Spirit might be poured out upon the gifts of bread and wine so that we might fully live into the holy mystery of the sacrament.

All of this points toward a reality that we aren't doing something grounded in the here and now—this is a precedential work that is alive and set apart. We are tying ourselves back to an ancient practice instructed by Jesus Christ with the original band of disciples in their gathered place in the upper room. The sacraments have been passed down thousands of years through many iterations of the Christian movement, but they are still deeply rooted in our life as the church. While we may divide ourselves over what qualifies as a sacrament between movements of the church, the truth is that our gatherings aren't rooted in a rich tradition set into play by the divine institution at its origination.

When we offer this sacrament in our space, we send out the needed element of bread and juice through a free subscription box that arrives in the mail each month. In nerdy fashion, it also comes with other snacks, Lego bricks, and an assortment of fun knickknacks. Not only have the elements been prayed over, but the box itself has been packed with care and shipped—a tactile act that is received in a tactile way.

Once it comes time for the actual liturgy, we invite all of the members of the community into a video call where we work through the text and blessing online. After the blessing, but before actually consuming the Communion elements, we have built a practice that reminds us that we are more than windows on a screen; we're bodies in the world. So, we built an app that has a big purple button that each person pushes down on their phone, which causes a number to go up with each new person clicking the button. That number that rises represents the present body of Christ, gathered together, even though physically apart. When we partake in this act, we aren't just enjoying bread and wine. We aren't just a club gathering and participating in a time together. We are a living organism, engaged in the past tradition and still today, growing ourselves into the ongoing evolution of what the early church instituted.

What I mean to say here is that we are something different entirely than any other sort of community-based gathering. There is something holy going on.

When Checkpoint first began to find its footing, this was something that we took very seriously. We didn't want to begin reaching nerds, geeks, and gamers online and lead them into feeling that we had hoodwinked them into joining a church when they believed they were just enjoying video games on the internet. We were unapologetic from our first day that we weren't trying to forge a fun community or a brand for a gaming streamer on Twitch. We were a church—through and through. We would be participating in that holy and divine nature that has been handed down. We would have fun along the way, sure. But our purpose and our goal was in line with the commission handed down from Jesus Christ.

AND ALSO ONLINE

All of these elements are demonstrably available through digital technology.

We evangelize through a number of tools on the internet. We engage routinely with people outside of our circle through sharing content on websites and applications such as YouTube, Instagram, and TikTok. On YouTube in particular, we have hundreds of comments from people outside of any traditional church structure affirming that our videos are reaching them and they are hearing the gospel for the first time, or at least for the first time since they left the church.

We are communal on Discord. We gather in what I refer to as a neo-monastic society of nonstop community. We share prayers and lunches. We care for one another and laugh together. We are aware of each other's lives—the woes and the joys. And we feel that we are an embodied gathering that many call their church.

We are discipleship-focused like any other church. We have Bible studies. We have sermons and conversations around them. We have spaces for spiritual questions. I attend to the pastoral care needs of the parish. We have hundreds, if not thousands, who are somewhere along a discipleship journey into our community.

And we are sacramental. This is the most controversial one. Following the approval of the episcopacy of The United Methodist Church, we observe Communion weekly. We have a well-considered liturgy of word and deed and embodied practices. We have a method behind the practice that includes elements distributed from our studio space in North Carolina that are distributed in subscription boxes worldwide. Baptism is a bridge we haven't quite yet crossed, but there are many out there who are doing baptisms online with trusted persons over a Zoom call. Or we may lean into the global Methodist connection of churches and have a local church near our parish member aid in the baptism process.

BUT WHAT ABOUT AI?

Perhaps the question leading your mind now is, What about AI? Hasn't the theme of the conversation been around artificial intelligence? Indeed, it has. But recall that artificial intelligence is just the latest outpouring of technological innovation. In reality, it has been around for decades. As we consider any connection between the church and our digital age, we are also talking about its relationship with artificial intelligence.

Even though I haven't used the phrase explicitly, what we call AI has been woven into these steps. What determines the algorithm and distributes our evangelistic efforts? AI. What fuels the bots for our Discord server? AI. What helps our discipleship content find its audience? AI.

Even our Communion practice was influenced and made better by artificial intelligence. We wanted to create an outward and visible sign of the inward and spiritual grace that is the digital connection. We developed an app, with the assistance of AI, that allows for our members to tangibly press a button online with a number keeping track of active users, a number that represents those gathered in the present body of Christ. I like to compare it to holding hands while taking Communion when we practice it. Without AI, communicating this number in this way would have been an undertaking beyond my capacity as a solo pastor.

However, this is not only a one-way relationship. Not only can artificial intelligence further the way that the church is visioned, but the church can have an impact on how we discuss AI. We should be having conversations as the church proper, whether that's The United Methodist Church or the broader Protestant movement or the church universal. Methodists have a tool called the Wesleyan Quadrilateral. This tool wasn't actually developed by John Wesley, but is a device crafted from the practices of Wesley by twentieth century theologian and Methodist scholar Albert Outler. This is a framework that we utilize for theological concerns, but it can be applied to any situation, really. More often than not, I find it being applied to social issues and sociological concerns.

For those unfamiliar, the Quadrilateral is a made up of four major lenses through which we view our discernment: Scripture, tradition, experience, and reason. For theological concerns, the most weight is placed on Scripture as the primary lens, so this is often referred to as a three-legged stool, with Scripture serving as the seat. It may be obvious, but by Scripture, we are referring to the Christian canon of Scripture contained within the Holy Bible. The other three may not be as obvious. When we look to our tradition, we look to the history of the church—as far back or recent as needed. We can look to John Wesley and the start of the Methodist movement, or Martin Luther, or the Council of Nicaea, or any pivotal moment establishing our tradition. Experience is a bit tricky and often controversial, but we must consider what wisdom we have in our own lives. Our own experiences and history shouldn't be the only lens we use; however, they are inseparable from our subconscious, and it would be better to use our experiences intentionally than to allow them to seep into our comprehension. And then reason is fairly straightforward—does it make logical sense? What role does rational thought play into our issues? Should we try to resolve an overflowing body of water with a drinking straw? Like tradition and experience, it ought not be the primary lens, because there should always be room for mystery and unknowing with the Divine in consideration.

So, let's play out an artificial intelligence concern and how it can be wrestled with using a tool from the established church. Should we allow for artificial intelligence to provide pastoral counseling to our parishioners? Scripture has little to say about pastoral care in a modern context, but we can glean some insights on the call of the leaders in the early church. First Peter 5:2 provides a framework for what an elder ought to do: "to tend the flock of God that is in your charge, exercising the oversight, not under compulsion but willingly, as God would have you do it, not for sordid gain but eagerly." Jesus commands in John 13:34 that we "love one another. Just as I have loved you, you also should love one another." These two sentiments point toward an active and participatory role in the work of caring for our parishioners. We ought not delegate this role out to an artificial intelligence for this reason alone; we are commissioned as leaders in the church to care for our flock, willingly and eagerly.

In our tradition, we might find some precedent for delegating out this role in specific scenarios. I was trained in seminary to be up front and transparent that my role is as a pastor, not a therapist. If I found a parishioner leaning on me as a therapist, I recommend outside services as assistance for that person in that specific scenario. But artificial intelligence is not a licensed therapist, either. We would vet any other resource, so we would be expected to analyze if AI could serve as a worthy therapist—and, by my estimation and the recommendations of the OpenAI company itself, it would not pass muster. For instance, there have been some upsetting situations where people have been utilizing ChatGPT as a therapist and have found their mental health only further deteriorating, sometimes to the extreme of suicide. Enough of these instances have led to OpenAI reining in the capacity of their AI to offer up mental health care.

I don't use AI as a therapist, but I do use it as a form of journaling my workdays in order to keep track of my energy expenditures. Am I using my time wisely or wasting days with menial tasks? I will prompt my chatbot with questions like that in order to better understand myself. However, I am not tying my emotional experience to the technology, I'm utilizing it as if it were a paper journal that I try to glean insights from, just more efficiently. On the other side, I have experienced the negative side of artificial intelligence, in particular with ChatGPT serving as a hype machine, only offering up platitudes and empty compliments. That is a worrying trait for a would-be therapist.

Does it even make sense for ChatGPT or some other interface to serve as a pastoral caregiver? One point that is radically in favor of artificial intelligence is its cost and widespread availability. It can always be accessed. As a pastor, I cannot say the same. ChatGPT can work effectively for $20 a month, or even for free. As someone supporting my family, I cannot say the same. Logically speaking, AI is certainly more cost- and time-effective than I am as a pastor. But what good is that time and cost if it's only offering hollow advice that wouldn't even be acceptable on its creator's own terms? Just because logic points toward some merits does not mean that this is a good choice.

Anyone using this framework would be able to discern that using artificial intelligence as a broad sweeping replacement for pastoral care is pure nonsense. This tool of the church is able to help pastors and church leaders to ask hard questions about applying this technology.

I wrote online about a use case for AI where a developer created an AI version of Jesus that would accept prayers and questions from those in the chat. Most of these comments were silly or intended to harass the AI, but some of them were concerningly vulnerable. They would offer up a prayer in earnest, as if this AI Jesus were actually Jesus. Sometimes, the AI would offer up pretty decent advice, but any of the harder questions would be dodged cleverly.

This is an indicator of why the relational work of the church is more important than ever. An AI Jesus is able to use Scripture in an innovative way to fake some decent answers, but it cannot really get to know the person on the other side of the chatbox. The work of the church is to remind itself of what it means to be the church. It is to realign us with the ecclesiological considerations that we often don't think about.

In the next chapter, we will take a look at what we vision as being the next steps forward for wisely incorporating technology like this into our church spaces. Crucially, we must first acknowledge that technology's impact upon the church has not fundamentally changed what makes church *church*. None of this progress has been done by artificial intelligence alone. But all of it is, in some way, made more realized through the application of the tool wisely.

CHAPTER 6

HUMAN-FORWARD THINKING

CHAPTER 6
Human-Forward Thinking

An early title of this book was, "The Holy Ghost in the Machine." The phrase "ghost in the machine" may not be familiar, but I first heard it (or a version of it) when I was a teenager and stumbled on an anime (a Japanese animation) called *Ghost in the Shell*. The series is a heart-wrenching one that explores transhumanism (human bodies amplified by machine parts) and the worth of the human mind in a world where human bodies are no longer necessary. At the time, I thought it was just an eerie and fascinating world to explore, but I learned that this transhumanist debate was not quite as modern as I might have thought.

The phrase "ghost in the machine" didn't start in anime. It was coined by the philosopher Gilbert Ryle, who was mocking René Descartes's idea that the mind and the body are separate substances, a concept more formally known as dualism. Ryle found the notion that the body and mind might be separate entities absurd. Decades later, science fiction authors nabbed the phrase to echo the human experience of discomfort with machines. The anime above took this idea and dramatized it. If your memories and thoughts are disconnected from your body, are you still yourself? What makes you human—your flesh or your mind? Writers and thinkers are still pondering this today. This is the stuff of science fiction that nerds like me live to read and explore. Like with AI, our imagination around these conversations is influenced dramatically by speculative science fiction.

In the last chapter, we explored some ways that my ministry might evoke this feeling from outsiders. There is a rightful skepticism toward a church that exists entirely online. Digital-first ministry feels at times like science fiction. I have a peer who espouses a prophetic vision that the *metaverse* is the future of the church. This so-called metaverse is a term used to describe the digitally interfaced realities that we share, most often attributed to the virtual reality habitats of headsets and avatars (I will have more to say about the metaverse later in this chapter). I can imagine that some look at our Discord server—which I fondly refer to as a neo-monastic society—and see a group of usernames who never leave each other alone, checking in on one another in prayer rooms and playing games in the early hours of the morning. What might they think about this vision of the church?

With AI, we now see glimpses of this discussion being made even more unsettling around us. We find ourselves at the forefront of something that feels an awful lot like science fiction—maybe even a dystopian world. From the uncanny by-products on generative video to the humanlike responses of ChatGPT, it's hard not to ascribe something to artificial intelligence that can come across as an echo of this fictional "ghost in the machine." It can feel like we aren't properly considering what makes us more human than machine.

We have people who are treating artificial intelligence models like therapy, talking to it and confessing deep, dark secrets. Many are finding the responses warm and empathetic (as they are trained to be). In mid-2025, OpenAI even performed a sort of "mind reset" on ChatGPT to become less accommodating to the delusions of its users who were creating unhealthy parasocial relationships. At the same time, as of this writing, OpenAI has also unveiled a customization feature for GPT-5 that allows the user to pick a "character" for the chat responses to follow— the Cynic persona, the Listener persona, the Robot persona, and the Nerd persona, undoubtedly with more on the way. The snuffing out of one form of parasocial relationship to be replaced with a more corporate approved one is bizarre and feels like the stuff of creative writing prompts. All of this echoes our recurring concern about anthropomorphizing AI as a disturbing trend.

In the light of this, we find ourselves at a point of tension. On one end, it can be easy to fall into a sort of despair over what feels inevitable. Like the ones who have had their parasocial relationships hit with a server reset at the drop of a hat, people are wont to turn to artificial intelligence for empathy. I've even experienced a form of this tension myself, utilizing ChatGPT as a living journal that I can take notes in during my workday for an evaluation at the end of each week. While I hold my boundaries pretty firm with any kind of artificial intelligence, it's undeniable that the responses *do* feel kind. They *do* feel empathetic.

However, on the other side of this paradigm, we have a sacred responsibility. Again, the creators of ChatGPT have clearly expressed that it isn't designed to be a therapist. They have limits on the advice that a chatbot can offer and are willing to pull the plug on those parasocialities without hesitation, recommending consultation before proceeding on any serious inquiries. And I know that the generated responses to my journal are less an empathetic friend and more an echo of my own sentiments, recapitulating the work I had already done, just cleaner.

Normally in a paradigmatic approach like this one, the opposite of despair would be represented by hope. But in our situation, I see the opposite of the despondence we see toward AI to be *responsibility*. It is our moral imperative that we pursue the best possible outcomes for the way that culture adopts and incorporates an inevitable artificial intelligence. This is the future of artificial intelligence and the church.

WHOSE BODY IS IT ANYWAY?

As Christians, we ask hard questions about what it means to be an embodied being. I briefly touched on the controversy around the embodiment of the members of the digital-first church plant that I serve, but we can't really explore the future without probing the issue a bit further. What is the nature of the body going forward? Genesis seems to point toward the body being vital for human life—we are dust brought to life when mixed with the breath of God. Many of the Old Testament characters appear to maintain their bodies when they die. In Genesis 5:24, Enoch is simply taken by God, never having to experience death. So, too, does Elijah get taken up to heaven in a whirlwind stirred up by a chariot of fire in 2 Kings 2:11. And in the New Testament, too, we see a resurrected Jesus whose body is a part of the story—John 20 shows us that Thomas must see and feel the holes in his hands.

But then, we also read the words of Paul, where he writes to the church in Corinth about the resurrected body. In chapter 15, he calls these questions foolish to begin with. We shouldn't assume that the body is important because, like a seed that is planted, the seed must die for the plant to grow. There are bodies in the heavens and bodies on the earth and when our earthly bodies are planted in the ground, they will be raised in glory. They are buried as natural human bodies but raised as spiritual ones. Is this metaphorical or literal? Is the transformation happening on this side of our lives or after an earthly demise? What do we do with this?

One of the biggest arguments that I hear against digital ministry is that it is not embodied, that there is some kind of dissonance between being a person with a body and a person using a computer or phone or tablet. I'll hear from folks who tell me that they just can't imagine feeling whole by engaging with others online. These two arguments often take place in the same breath, but they are saying quite different things. One is arguing that they aren't able to experience engaging relationships online. The other is arguing that the very act of being online is not capable of being embodied. One is a preference; the other is opinion paraded as fact. I disagree with the claim that we somehow become magically disembodied when we are typing on a keyboard. I am still in my own skin and fully capable of sensations as I swipe across a screen or hear someone's voice from my headphones. While it may not be the preference of many, that doesn't negate the capacity to have online embodied connection.

Consider again the work of Paul in writing letters to the early churches. He writes in 1 Corinthians 5:3 that he may be absent from them in body and yet present with them in spirit. There is something tangible happening in our communications—even from long distances. Paul didn't cease being Paul when he wrote letters. I don't shed my body when I post a video; I send a piece of myself, mediated through wires and screens, bits and bytes. I believe that the call for the church here is not to dismiss the digital space as being disembodied, but to ask more honest questions, like how we might live faithfully as embodied people *within* new digital spaces. This is the better vision for the future of technology in the church.

No one is denying the importance of the body in our lives. I think of the Gospel of John's epic opening refrain, which is hauntingly beautiful: "In the beginning was the Word, and the Word was with God, and the Word was God" (John 1:1). This is a retelling of the origin of humanity from Genesis, with the God-man Jesus at the center in this recitation. The Gospel writer continues, "And the Word became flesh and lived among us, and we have seen his glory, the glory as of a father's only son, full of grace and truth" (John 1:14). In this we see the culmination of the Genesis story resulting in the Word being enfleshed and embodied. In Christ, we see the power of our bodies. We understand that there is something happening when we acknowledge the flesh that we inhabit. It was important enough that Jesus needed to incarnate—there needed to be a body. Digital embodiment is not shedding this reality but celebrating it in a new way.

I would also be remiss not to mention a darker side of our bodies being involved in the digital parts of our lives. Not only do we actually feel in general, but we also particularly feel the hurt and the stress of this digital reality in our bodies. A part of our embodied nature is also the capacity to experience pain. We see the effects of this on a daily basis. I have a permanent indentation on my pinky finger from the way that I hold my smartphone whenever I text on my phone messenger app. If I don't take frequent breaks from screen time, then I will develop a headache—my body will tell me I've spent too long in my stead. My in-ear headphones have a feature now that will ping me with a notification if I've been craning my neck down looking at my phone for too long. In a more pressing example, I will feel real anxiety from uncomfortable interactions online. I will feel real stress and shame for negative comments or anonymous commenters lambasting my appearance or thoughts.

We cannot have a real conversation about technological health until we acknowledge that our bodies are very deeply involved in this part of our lives. And we cannot just go outside and be on our digital devices less. This approach is a temporary solution at best. Even in our best attempts to regulate phone use in school settings, we are only delaying the inevitable and pushing away our young people in our desire to control. It is better to educate on healthy practices than to assume everyone is an addict who cannot regulate technology use.

Thus, when we clear out the misunderstanding that our digital presence is disembodied, we can once again celebrate the importance of the bodies that we inhabit. Artificial intelligence is simply not embodied. It should not be given this human quality. It is a creation. It is a technology. One can choose flowery language or technical language, but that doesn't change the root definition of the thing being outside the realm of embodiment. There is no amount of empathetic consideration that can change this reality. If we are losing to artificial intelligence in the field of empathy, then

I encourage us to see that as a failure on our part, not a success on the part of AI. We must do better and be better as the exemplars of the radical empathy that Christ showed as an embodied, incarnate being who modeled for us "the way and the truth and the life" (John 14:6).

STOP BEFORE IT STARTS

We have an opportunity at this moment to step into the evolving landscape and be a part of shaping it. If, as we've explored, AI is somehow more effective at providing warmth and empathy, then we must adapt as embodied people online to provide a better experience of empathy than a disembodied machine. As people with bodies online, we should be asking how we must better use our bodies to do things that artificial intelligence is not capable of doing. Try as they might, by their own definition, there is no way for an artificial intelligence to transcend the *artificial* part—we are still the flesh and blood of the internet.

I believe that this can be done by what we do preemptively and what we do in real time with artificial intelligence.

On the preparatory front, we should be considerate of how we intend to implement artificial intelligence in what I am proposing as a human-forward approach. What if we only deploy AI in ways that increase the opportunities for humans to offer embodied presence? What if we intentionally develop a practice of using AI to free up administrative hours in exchange for relational hours? I believe that AI is at its best when it is viewed as an augmenter, not a replacement or a full solution. As someone who led worship for several years, I can recall just how much of my time was spent coming up with the schedule for our myriad of volunteers. What if AI were able to generate a list beyond a randomizer? It could choose songs that are better tuned to whoever is on the schedule for that week, rather than the time it takes to administrate that work. More time could be spent with the team themselves, bonding and learning new music instead. Still, we should be clear about who is in control of the way that we implement technology.

Consider the errors of our past with letting technology run unwatched—the slightest dissonance can be catastrophic. Online, we are currently experiencing the explosion of culture wars. Ideologies are being shared in echo chambers that are exacerbated by the algorithmic feeds that continue to offer up the latest plate of bias. When we let technology shape us instead of the reverse, we find ourselves at the manipulative beck and call of the driving factors of capitalism only seeking attention that leads to more dollars. The social media bubble comes closer to popping every day, as many find the purer feeds of Discord and RSS more appealing and less manipulated. We missed the chance with social media, but we can still play a part in the evolution of AI. Leading with human-forward techniques will be the safest way to explore how the technology can spur us forward.

An example of this might be seen with a tool like Grammarly. This is a sort of artificial intelligence that is applied to works that we have already written, with an eye tuned to aiding in the proper usage of grammatical and rhetorical techniques. Who hasn't wondered when the correct time to use "whom" might be? In this instance, one isn't turning over the act of writing itself to artificial intelligence. The writing has been done by the creative brain and then the details are sorted out by the helpful AI. Augmentation, not replacement. This is what I mean by human-forward.

An example of technology-forward would be the negative example listed above—have the AI write the entire piece for you. The reality is that it isn't honest. It's bearing a false witness to the work we put forward. We shouldn't let the tools use us, but we should discern when the proper time is to let them augment our work.

Another preemptive step revolves around the pressing ecological cost of data centers and the demand they place upon water consumption. We haven't explored this aspect of AI much in this book, but it takes a vast amount of energy to run the server farms that prop up this wide-reaching industry. That energy generates heat, which must be cooled with water. We should always be aware of Romans 8:22-23: "We know that the whole creation has been groaning together as it suffers together the pains of labor, and not only the creation, but we ourselves, who have the first fruits of the Spirit, groan inwardly while we wait for adoption, the redemption of our bodies." In order to love God and neighbor, we shouldn't wait complacently but redeem the earth in the ways that we might be able to in this present time, bringing about the kingdom of heaven here on earth. We should set up clear boundaries for what is a worthy use of artificial intelligence. And to be blunt, we should take that same approach with any kind of technology we implement. We should strive to use technology when it brings about good and multiplies love and justice, but steer away from burning resources for vanity projects. All things in excess bring harm, as the adage goes.

And then we ought to be actively engaged with artificial intelligence in an intentional way to shape the narrative as it develops. Many models are trained on our usage of them. Our inputs, our interactions, our usage . . . we should be signaling to the algorithm what is a healthy use of these models. We should set clear and transparent boundaries of what is and isn't appropriate when it comes to generative practices. This is equally true for the eyes that we have watching us that are not artificial. I am all too painfully cognizant of my daughters watching me use (or choose not to use) artificial intelligence in daily practice. In our congregations, we should be modeling healthy boundaries and best techniques for not becoming dependent on the technology but only allowing it to be used to maximum efficacy.

THE VALUE OF TRUST

One of the more pressing concerns for the future of AI technology is in our willingness to use it for further division in our culture. Consider again our opening chapter—in 2020, artificial intelligence was new and unknown to most outside of the tech enthusiasts of the world. Just a few years later, it's prevalent in every household, classroom, and office. Out of all the spaces that have seen a rise, the ones that seem to be having the most trouble with moderating the technology have been those in education. Teachers have been shouting from the rooftops their frustration about the widespread use of artificial intelligence for cheating on assignments. Like anyone curious about the field, we see that the evolution happens so rapidly, there is really no way to catch up to the pace of it.

It's been fascinating to see the many ways that this has reverberated into potential halfway solutions. I've seen teachers hiding invisible letters on their rubrics in order to give ChatGPT (or whatever model the student is using) secret instructions as a giveaway that the student cheated. In one of the most ironic twists, others are importing papers to another artificial intelligence that can provide an analysis of if it believes the paper to have been written by AI. These are notoriously problematic and seem to not work most of the time, falsely flagging legitimate work. Deans of schools are threatening expulsion and permanent record demerits for students who utilize this untrustworthy technology. Companies like OpenAI and Google are being pressured on all sides to offer up solutions to the problems—tracking the word documents to see the pace that the student is writing at or if they are just copy-pasting from AI.

When it generates text, ChatGPT is prone to using the em dash (—) very frequently to set off ideas. Many are now skeptical of any paper that utilizes the em dash—properly or improperly. Given my proclivity to use such punctuation, this author would be quite unlucky in a scholastic setting! In fact, I've wrestled a bit with others who find my writing to feel like artificial intelligence. We are training a cavalcade of shrewd private investigators, seeking out every instance of "it's not this, it's that" and list of three things. I've seen creative people putting out their best work only to have it brushed aside as nothing more than artificial intelligence. This can be frustrating and disheartening in a world with enough challenges for the independent creator.

In the midst of all of this, I'm reminded of our earlier conversations around those who are "never AI" people. These are those who will never consider any use of AI to be acceptable, choosing to instead cease support for anyone willing to explore the tool. This is no more than a subset of the cancellation obsession on the internet, but it should be something that we are quite concerned with in the church. To me, it is most concerning that we have this widespread doubt in our fellow human beings. It's as if our default setting—even in academia—is to presume that no one is trustworthy. We are all guilty until proven innocent by avoiding every em dash.

This is not how we are meant to live as Christians. This is not loving our neighbor.

Our default is meant to be rooted deeply in love, not disdain. We are people of hope and loving-kindness, not distrust and retribution. In 1 Corinthians 13:6-7, Paul commends us to a stance of love that "does not rejoice in wrongdoing but rejoices in the truth. It bears all things, believes all things, hopes all things, endures all things." We are not opposed to truth and justice, but our posture is one of hope first, belief first, endurance first. We approach one another with grace and welcome. In the Gospel of John, Christ holds his critics to a higher calling: "Do not judge by appearances, but judge with right judgment" (7:24). Again, we are not called away from judgment and justice, but we ought not to allow our gut instinct to be cruelty and punishment. In a confrontation, we should not be cutting people off at their first offense—let alone a *perceived* offense. This is a far cry from the radical love we're called to exhibit.

I feel a deep empathy with the students of our current time. It was challenging enough as a student of the '00s and '10s with the feeling of pressure by digital technology setting us to a higher standard, or the outright bias against the use of it. I can recall when Wikipedia, the encyclopedia of the internet, was considered to be the most egregious tool ever created. I was led to believe that people would intentionally add lies to Wikipedia pages while twisting their stereotypical villain mustache, giggling at their feat of fooling some high schooler writing about Mark Twain. I once had a professor who threatened to fail anyone who cited Wikipedia. Did this lead to our avoidance of Wikipedia? Not at all. We found that the sources at the bottom of Wikipedia were exceptional primary sources that took a dramatically shorter amount of time to find. So, we would use Wikipedia to find our sources, rather than make it our source—one step removed from just using the site as the full citation. Was this the result that the professors wanted? Likely not, but that is what technology does best. It provides a new toolbox. A new framework that might shift the paradigm into a new way of doing things, often much faster than before. Thanks to that pressure, we did discover the importance of using technology, not being used by it.

I'm not trying to suggest that the students using artificial intelligence for an easy A should be let off the hook. There should still be expectations placed on those pursuing higher education—but they should be fair and equitable, not harsh and unreasonable. Frankly, those in positions of authority should be doing their due diligence to understand the tools in order to provide fair frameworks for students to work within. I understand that the pace of AI development makes this a challenging, if not impossible. But is it really fair to put the pressure on those seeking out education instead? If we really want to see what AI is capable of shaping in the future, we should allow the students enough room to play and enough constraints to innovate.

All of this is rooted in my Wesleyan heritage and John Wesley's belief that there is no holiness but social holiness. In social holiness, there is a certain underlying requirement that trust be built among people. In order for Wesley's societies to work, there needed to be a level of trusting groups who could lean on one another in community. If we continue down this road of division around technology and artificial intelligence, then we will be eroding the pursuit of holiness that is only made possible by our relationships with one another in Christian community. This is also why transparency is a core facet of my rules for proper AI implementation. We can earn that trust by assuring our own honesty and expecting the same of others.

A METAVERSAL TRUTH

We haven't gone into great detail about the metaverse in this book, but we have certainly skirted around it—especially when talking about the digital-first ministry of the church that I serve. For those unfamiliar, *metaverse* is a term coined by Neal Stephenson in his dystopian cyberpunk novel *Snow Crash*. The book was published in 1992 and features many elements of our current digital age in an uncanny way. It was seen as a sort of prophetic speculation on how technology might form. Despite offering a bleak view of how we might find ourselves involved in the digital space, many aspirational developers took the ideas of this book and other science fiction writers into their career, forging those bits of fiction into real life.

Metaverse, as it is used today, is a somewhat difficult concept to define. Its most important aspect is an interconnected universe of digital spaces. Think of a sort of immersive and extensive virtual reality—an expansive digital space where people can interact in a variety of ways with a digital environment and digital representations of real people. If you're familiar with computer games, people have likened *The Sims*, *Minecraft*, and *Roblox* to the metaverse since they are places where you can engage in a variety of activities—learning and teaching, buying and selling, playing and competing, talking and sharing. Some readers may have heard the term when the company that owns Facebook (now named Meta, a signal to its new direction) introduced a metaverse concept of their own in 2021.

What started as a sort of buzzword in an era of the internet has evolved into a robust industry of virtual reality headsets and augmented reality glasses and spaces inhabited by avatars of real-life people, not just fictional characters. Even the term *avatar* is one that was co-opted from an earlier time but is now made commonplace in a world of online connection.

While the term metaverse is more often interpreted to be referring to the phenomenon of physical bodies interacting in virtual spaces, I see the *metaverse* as a step in the evolutionary chain of how we interact as people. For now, we log on to a virtual hub on a VR headset and affix the clunky hardware to our heads and try not to drum up too much motion sickness as we interact online. But think of the less obvious ways that we are doing that without the heavy hardware—when we gather on a Discord server and leave it up on a second monitor at work, when we direct message rendered avatars of ourselves making silly expressions in response to our friends, or when we offer a hugging emoji in response to a heartbreaking prayer request shared on our loved one's feed. These are less overt, but unquestionably ways that we are interacting through a digital interface. These are, in a sense, metaversal interactions. We are connecting via digital means, even in the worlds beyond our screens. And these interactions are only getting more common, more natural, and more invasive.

My prediction is that our metaverse future looks less like VR headsets and full immersion and more like a Discord server of people that see each other as a neo-monastic society: a group of people who may have never shaken physical hands, but are unquestionably tied together through daily interactions and bonds built around pixels and megabytes.

I've mentioned several times before that artificial intelligence is much older than we might believe and already woven into many of our systems. This is especially true of our metaverse interactions. Facebook is powered by AI systems. Video games are utilizing AI. No doubt we would find many AI processes interwoven in virtual reality. It's been said that the metaverse is our future, and artificial intelligence is an indelible part of that technology. If the church wishes to remain connected to the lives of our communities in the future, we must be aware of what it means to bring Christ to the metaverse—and that means considering AI just as well.

MORE THAN A GHOST

I began this chapter by sharing the original title of *Holy Ghost in the Machine*. I enjoy the allusion to a divine sort of mystery that happens within technology, but there is an important boundary set by the ideas posited in this book of how God interplays with the machine, rather than inhabiting the thing. God is not the machine, nor is the machine a god. The church should be less interested in seeing some kind of divine inspiration from code and numbers and learning models and more interested in how God uses technology at all. We are tasked with prudent and grace-filled application of technology like artificial intelligence into our ministries, not haphazard and wanton permission-giving toward machines with inherent biases and shortcomings.

However, I think it's equally important that we not call this work *God* or *the Machine* . . . the machine is not an either/or situation. All of this points toward that same pressing inevitability from the start of this chapter: Artificial intelligence is here, and it is only going to continue being a part of our lives. It can likely research more effectively, schedule better, and write faster—but it cannot be better neighbors. It cannot be the embodied people online. It cannot be considered people at all.

We aren't called to out-innovate Silicon Valley; we're called to implement that technology in ways that embody Christ. It's not in our mission to be known by our innovation, but by our love. In the age of machines, let us not strive to be known for clever prompts, but for faithfully loving God and neighbor.

CONCLUSION

Building a Better World with Wisdom

As we come to a close, there are several things to keep in mind. Most pressing, the specific details of the technologies we have discussed might be dramatically different by the time you read this book. With the rapid advancement of artificial intelligence, it's likely that something has changed from the time I started writing this book to the time I wrote this chapter, so it's even more likely to shift in months and years from this being published. I have attempted to keep this in mind as I've written.

To prove my point, since I started writing this manuscript, OpenAI revealed GPT-5, and it changed everything about the way that users control it. They turned their product from being highly customizable with many various models to select and put them all into one smart flagship model that would decide what to do depending on your prompt. If it's an easier task, it uses a lighter model. If it's a more complex task, it would pull in the big model. What used to be a choice of the user was obfuscated by the AI itself. I'm no Nostradamus, but I assume that this won't work and will likely be adjusted into something in between, allowing the user to customize again in the near future.

Consider the company Perplexity, a privately held software company that has put their focus on crafting an internet browser that is powered by generative models of artificial intelligence. In the midst of writing this book, they put in an unsolicited bid to buy out Google Chrome from Alphabet for $34.5 billion. For those unfamiliar, Chrome is a widely adopted internet browser, considered to be an industry standard. Most browsers that aren't called Google Chrome still use a framework called Chromium. This is an absurd move on behalf of Perplexity with huge consequences if it actually goes anywhere in the world of massive technological acquisitions. This is akin to the new kid on the block trying to usurp the very top slot in the neighborhood hierarchy. A company founded in 2022 has risen fast enough to offer a purchase of the most established web browser from one of the most established tech companies in the world. That should illustrate just how unpredictable this world can be. But we shouldn't have to predict the next move to prepare ourselves for how to best respond to any change these companies can make.

This is a fast-moving industry, and the church has historically not been the fastest moving thing around. But consider again our progenitor Bezalel—a historic technologist! Consider again our epistle-writing Paul—an adaptive mover and shaker of a new technology in an ancient era. Consider again our denominational father John Wesley and the apt use of the pamphlet as a means to delivering the good news in ways we had never thought possible. We now find ourselves in yet another moment of opportunity to change the way that ministry is done, while our message remains unchanged.

Before anything else, Christians must start with the understanding that much of our imagination comes from within science fiction. Yet it's better to understand that artificial intelligence isn't really science fiction's magical and foreboding predictions—it is much more centered around the generation of text and imagery. While the church cannot opt out of this shift—no more than we could the printing press or the internet—artificial intelligence need not be the boogeyman. We should be at the front of this, naming our own terms, limits, and boundaries with theological and pastoral discernment.

We can do this important work because we understand our role as stewards of creation, as echoes of the creator God, specifically commissioned to guide these things forward so that human beings are held in places of dignity, with their craft and call honored. We know this not only from a theological level, but also a practical one. We've seen how technology has accelerated the church, but only when used as a distinct tool that is utilized wisely to provide more free time for presence, a widening of accessibility, and more efficient ministry planning; we shouldn't replace relationships but rather allow for time to deepen them.

All of this is done with a deep-rooted deference to our ethical sensibilities. Ethics must be the engine driving this movement forward, or else we are putting the cart before the horse, so to speak.

We know now that artificial intelligence is not without its biases, plagiaristic tendencies, hallucinations, deepfakes, and convincing faux empathy. We need to be up-front with our guardrails for how we implement AI into our spaces in ways that seek justice, love mercy, and walk humbly with God (Micah 6:8).

Even with ethics in our sight, we shouldn't dismiss technology out of our confusion around digital ministry. In fact, we should allow those working in this cutting-edge ministry to speak to the ways that this technology can better shape the historic practice of discipleship into our modern understanding of church. Artificial intelligence, like any other technology, should support our embodied ecclesiology.

And finally, we ought to go forward with hope and take responsibility for the way that artificial intelligence will be shaped in the coming years. Religion is a major facet of cultural life, and the way that we approach these matters will shape the way that our communities do the same.

My goal with these chapters has been to zoom out a bit and show the broader perspective of how we can apply artificial intelligence in our context. I've attempted to share a possible ethic, laying some policy foundations that you may choose to use in your local church setting. I hoped to clear up some misconceptions about what artificial intelligence actually is and why it's so challenging to many people. I have tried to establish what role the church ought to play in this digital world we're inhabiting. And perhaps I've set a tone for how we can all move into human-forward thinking in an era that seems to be quickly careening against digital liturgy. At the start of our journey together, I said that I wished to toe the line between skeptic and optimist. While it can be challenging not to fall into either camp when considering certain factors, I believe that the best way for a Christian leader to carry the mantle forward in this vein is with a healthy dose of both. I've read quite a bit of the opinions on both sides of this spectrum. Often I agree with both of them too. The most challenging on each side are those who attempt to demonize the other. Those who are never-AI and passionate about writing off the AI enthusiast are troubling—if for no other reason than the ominous issues and concerns they are effectively allowing to deepen and expand.

The truth is that the AI enthusiast *needs* the skeptic. How else can we hope to find boundaries and ethics in the midst of that? On the other hand, those who are so AI-positive that they refuse to consider anyone who won't utilize the tool (the phrase "get in or get left behind" rings out here) are also troubling, especially if they are Christian. There is nothing less loving of our neighbor than leaving them behind, even if it's only in our imagination. The AI skeptic also *needs* the enthusiast. We can't expect AI to go the way of cryptocurrency and find a lane that doesn't impact our daily lives. AI is too effervescent; it's too involved in our lives already. At our best, we can view AI as the tool that I believe it to be. And a tool needs strict guardrails. But a tool also is unquestionably useful. To walk that line is the discerning path of the wise leader.

When we consider the technological advancements of society and their impact on the church, it's less about the tool itself and more about how we properly discern its role in Kingdom-building. Does this tool help us to better love God? Does this tool help us to better love our neighbor? These are core and widely applicable,

Conclusion

even if GPT-7 enters the market tomorrow. These are the questions we considered as we began our time together. But I hope that they don't begin and end with this book. I hope that we can frame our interactions with the digital world between these concepts. May we, as the church, rise to this challenge with the creativity of our Creator, the humility of servants, and the wisdom of the Holy Spirit as our guide.